Lebanese Historical Thought in the Eighteenth Century

This study of Lebanese historical thought and its role in national identity formation in the eighteenth century focuses on a sample of historians, mainly Christians, who lived and wrote during the Shihabi Emirate from 1697 till the Egyptian invasion in 1831.

These historians, who represent different trends in historical writing, were able to develop the idea of Lebanon as a unique entity and as a haven and to underline its specificity and distinctiveness. With a focus on primary sources, this book endeavors to penetrate into the main concerns and ways of thinking at this time when a Lebanese identity started to bloom. In doing so, it discovers a neglected century as a fruitful and rich period in the history of Lebanon and a prelude to nineteenth-century awakening.

This book will be of interest to scholars of the history and historiography of Lebanon and the Middle East, with relevance for specialized courses in the fields of history and historiography at universities.

Hayat El Eid Bualuan is a lecturer at the American University of Beirut.

Routledge Approaches to History

47 **How to Write About the Holocaust**
The Postmodern Theory of History in Praxis
Theodor Pelekanidis

48 **The Politics of Time in China and Japan**
Back to the Future
Viren Murthy

49 **Nation and the Writing of History in China and Britain, 1880-1930**
Asier H. Aguirresarobe

50 **Ideas and Methodologies in Historical Research**
Vladimer Luarsabishvili

51 **Clarifying the Past**
Understanding Historical Commissions in Conflicted and Divided Societies
Cira Palli-Asperó

52 **Combining Political History and Political Science**
Towards a New Understanding of the Political
Edited by Carlos Domper Lasús and Giorgia Priorelli

53 **Lebanese Historical Thought in the Eighteenth Century**
Hayat El Eid Bualuan

For more information about this series, please visit: https://www.routledge.com/Routledge-Approaches-to-History/book-series/RSHISTHRY

Lebanese Historical Thought in the Eighteenth Century

Hayat El Eid Bualuan

NEW YORK AND LONDON

First published 2023
by Routledge
605 Third Avenue, New York, NY 10158

and by Routledge
4 Park Square, Milton Park, Abingdon, Oxon, OX14 4RN

Routledge is an imprint of the Taylor & Francis Group, an informa business

© 2023 Taylor & Francis

The right of Hayat El Eid Bualuan to be identified as author of this work has been asserted in accordance with sections 77 and 78 of the Copyright, Designs and Patents Act 1988.

All rights reserved. No part of this book may be reprinted or reproduced or utilised in any form or by any electronic, mechanical, or other means, now known or hereafter invented, including photocopying and recording, or in any information storage or retrieval system, without permission in writing from the publishers.

Trademark notice: Product or corporate names may be trademarks or registered trademarks, and are used only for identification and explanation without intent to infringe.

ISBN: 978-0-367-90262-9 (hbk)
ISBN: 978-1-032-45583-9 (pbk)
ISBN: 978-1-003-02343-2 (ebk)

DOI: 10.4324/9781003023432

Typeset in Times New Roman
by KnowledgeWorks Global Ltd.

Contents

Introduction   1

1 **Chronicle Writing**   5
   1.1   *Rufail Karameh el Himsi (1730–1800)* 5
   1.2   *Antonios Abu Khattar al Aynturini (d. 1821)* 10
   1.3   *Haydar Ibn Rida al Rukayni (1711–1784)* 13
   1.4   *Concluding Remarks* 15
   Acknowledgments 16

2 **Neo-Chroniclers**   19
   2.1   *Hanania al Munayyir (1756–1823)* 19
   2.2   *Niqula al Turk (1763–1828)* 26
   2.3   *Haidar Ahmad al Shihabi (1761–1835)* 31
   Acknowledgments 37

3 **Biographical Writing**   42
   3.1   *Autobiography: Abdallah Qarali (1674–1742)* 42
   3.2   *Biography: Abbud al Sabbagh (d. 1799)* 49
   Acknowledgments 53

4 **Apologetic History: The Maronite Question**   57
   4.1   *Yusuf Simaan al Simani (1687–1768)* 57
   4.2   *Yuhanna al Ujaimi (1724–1785)* 59

Conclusion   65

Index   70

Introduction

In his book, *Arabic Historical Thought in the Classical Period*, Professor Tarif al Khalidi writes: "Historians may be informative in either of two different ways. For what they may or may not tell us about the past or for what they tell us about thinking about the past."[1]

My own interest is centered in this book on this aspect of historiography where the different historians of Lebanon enable us to fathom the eighteenth century in its political, historical, intellectual, and social aspects and to penetrate the reality of that century as a basis for the awakening of the nineteenth century and not a period of stagnation and decay.

Historiographical studies can be undertaken as means and ends at the same time. On the one hand, they can reveal something about the state of the historical discipline itself; on the other, they can be treated as a device for shedding additional light on the intellectual or sociopolitical climate of a given period.[2]

The historians of the eighteenth century, whether chroniclers or neo-chroniclers, biographers, autobiographers, or historians of dialectics, reflected the society they were living in, its concerns and its mode of thinking enabling us to penetrate deeply into that century, an unfathomed and controversial period in the history of Lebanon. These historians, mostly Christians, who were preoccupied with the news of the Church, the source of their identity, and the social, political, and intellectual history of Lebanon, reflect the mode of thinking in that century and constitute at the same time a basis for the cultural and social awakening of the nineteenth century not only in Lebanon, but in *Bilād al Shām* in general.

The reason why more Lebanese Christians have delved into history than non-Christians – Sunnis, Shiites, and Druzes – may be understood in the light of three factors: (a) Christians, particularly Catholics and Maronites, had an edge in education by having the chance to

DOI: 10.4324/9781003023432-1

2 *Introduction*

study in Rome and Europe; (b) Muslims were interested in a wider history comprising Islamic history and this was already explored in depth by other historians in the wider Arab world; and (c) Maronites, in a tightly knit community around the patriarch, forged an identity of their own and the historians of that period embarked on studying this phenomenon.

Our approach to the eighteenth century is through a few historians whose writings reflected historical thinking in that period and at the same time presented an image of society in its intellectual, cultural, social, political, and religious thinking.[3] We will not focus here on what the historians relate about the past, but on what they tell us about thinking about the past. This is how we will be provided with the details to fathom the intellectual atmosphere in the eighteenth century and come to a better understanding not only of the basis and the edifice of the nineteenth-century awakening, but also to the idea of a Lebanese identity which was thriving throughout the ages and blossomed in the eighteenth century.[4]

We approach the eighteenth century by analyzing the writings of the historians first as chroniclers in relating the various events, political, social, and intellectual. We focus here not only on high society and its concerns, but also on local history where the preoccupation of the people introduces us to their daily lives and their mode of thinking. It is in this way that we approach the society from its different angles: the ruling strata – whether in politics or in religion – and the lives of the ordinary people and their allegiance to their locality.

Our approach to the eighteenth century is in the realm of biographical writing too. Here, we start with autobiography where the historian concentrates on describing himself, his life and feelings, the society he was living in, the personal ordeals he passed through, and the experiences he encountered in shaping himself and his society.

Moving to biographical writing, we encounter the historian relating the life of a ruler and his associates, introducing us to the society in its political, social, and regional aspects. It is here that one gets through biography not only the life of an individual, but also a glimpse of important historical events of the period which in most of its parts shaped historical thinking.

It is then that the crowning mode of writing comes into the picture when writing history develops into what is called apologetic history presented in the controversy of the period concerning the Maronite question and their allegiance to Rome. The historians here quote different sources and resort to logic to prove their point.

Introduction 3

This study then has two purposes: understanding the eighteenth century through the writings of these historians as a basis for both Lebanese identity and the awakening of the nineteenth century and not a period of stagnation as was commonly understood.⁵ Second, delving into the methods of these historians as chroniclers, autobiographers, biographers, and lastly historians of apologetics will open before us different trends concerning a century rich in its achievements and a valuable edifice to understand the following centuries.

Historiographical studies and the awakening of the eighteenth century in Lebanon and Bilad al Sham have induced me to numerous projects on the subject throughout the years. It is here that I would like to mention that a few sections in this book appeared in previous articles in different journals.⁶ It is in this study that I place these articles in a coherent whole to draw conclusions concerning Lebanese historical thinking in the eighteenth century.

I would like to conclude by mentioning the inspiring academic atmosphere at the American University of Beirut and particularly the support of Dr. Nader el Bizri, whose devotion to learning and research was continuously an example to follow. I would like especially to acknowledge the meticulous help and commitment of Dr. Scott Parker, whose help and concern while editing the manuscript added more precision to the task. Last, but not least, special thanks to my two sons and their spouses, Said and Samira, Ramzi and Ghada, for their continuous support.

Notes

1. Tarif Khalidi, *Arabic Historical Thought in the Classical Period* (Cambridge: Cambridge University Press, 1994), xi.
2. On the writing of history, see Ernst Breisach, *Historiography: Ancient, Medieval, and Modern* (Chicago, IL: University of Chicago Press, 1994); R.G. Collingwood, *The Idea of History* (Oxford: Oxford University Press, 1994); S. Kracaur, *History, the Last Things before the Last* (Princeton, NJ: Marcus Weiner Publishers, 1995); Carl E. Schorske, *Thinking with History* (Princeton, NJ: Princeton University Press, 1998).
3. The historians were situated within the century they were writing in. I followed the date of their death as much as possible to solve the problem of time delimitation for those who lived both in the eighteenth and in the nineteenth centuries at the time of the Shihabi Emirate from 1697 until the Egyptian invasion in 1831. See: Kamal Salibi, *The Modern History of Lebanon* (New York, NY: Caravan Books, 1999), 18–39.
4. Meir Zamir states the following: "It is doubtful whether any other country in the Middle East apart from Egypt can claim such a long, continuous history as a political entity. A truly Lebanese entity, the Imarah emerged in the late sixteenth and early seventeenth centuries

during the reign of Fakhr al Din II." "Within the limits of this territory an evolving form of political authority has continued without interruption from the early seventeenth century to our own time giving Lebanon a separate and distinct identity." Quoted in Salibi, *The Modern History of Lebanon*, xiii.
5 Bruce Masters, The View from the Province, "*Syrian Chronicles of the Eighteenth Century*" JOAS. 114/3 (1994), 353–362; Thomas Philip, "*Class Community and Arab Historiography in the Early Nineteenth Century: The Dawn of a New Era*," *IJMES*, 16 (1984): 161–175.
6 "Rufail Karameh al Himsi (1730–1800) and His Hawadith Lubnan wa Suriya," *Parole de L'Orient* 27 (2002): 133–146; "Abbud al Sabbagh and His Biography of Daher al 'Umar," *Parole de L'Orient* 24 (1999): 339–356; and "A Vision of a Historian: Hanania al Munayyir in *al Durr al Marsuf fi Hawadith al Shuf*," *Collectanea Christiana Orientalia* 13 (2017): 1–131.

References List

Breisach, Ernst. *Historiography: Ancient, Medieval, and Modern*. Chicago, IL: University of Chicago Press, 1994.
Bualuan, Hayat. "A Vision of a Historian: Hanania al Munayyir in *al Durr al Marsuf fi Hawadith al Shuf*." *Collectanea Christiana Orientalia* 13 (2017): 1–131.
———. "Abbud al Sabbagh and His Biography of Daher al 'Umar." *Parole de L'Orient* 24 (1999): 339–356.
———. "Rufail Karameh al Himsi (1730–1800) and His *Hawadith Lubnan wa Suriya*." *Parole de L'Orient* 27 (2002): 133–146.
Collingwood, Robin George. *The Idea of History*. Oxford: Oxford University Press, 1994.
Khalidi, Tarif. *Arabic Historical Thought in the Classical Period*. Cambridge: Cambridge University Press, 1994.
Kracaur, Sigfried and Krtisteller Paul Oscar. *History, the Last Things before the Last*. Princeton, NJ: Marcus Weiner Publishers, 1995.
Masters, Bruce. "The View from the Province: Syrian Chronicles of the Eighteenth Century." *Journal of Oriental and African Studies* 114/3 (1994): 353–362.
Philip, Thomas. "Class Community and Arab Historiography in the Early Nineteenth Century: The Dawn of a New Era." *International Journal of Middle Eastern Studies* 16 (1984): 161–175.
Salibi, Kamal. *The Modern History of Lebanon*. New York, NY: Caravan Books, 1999.
Schorske, Carl E. *Thinking with History*. Princeton, NJ: Princeton University Press, 1998.

1 Chronicle Writing

Chroniclers throughout different ages have followed time sequence in relating events.[1] The word "Chronicle" derives from *Chronos*, a Greek word meaning time, and is used to indicate consecutive historical information without any link except time sequence. This does not mean that one can differentiate completely between narrative history and analytic history. There always exists constant overlapping between relating the events, thinking about the events, or discovering their significance. In fact, whether the historian's aim is to relate the events or think about their significance, through these writings one can always discover the society these historians were living in, its preoccupations, way of living and mode of thinking to be enabled to come to a better understanding of the century they were living in and to trace the development of thinking throughout the ages.

1.1 Rufail Karameh el Himsi (1730–1800)

We start with Rufail Karameh al Himsi, who related the events in their time sequence and as with other chroniclers was merely preoccupied with what concerned these chroniclers most: the weather, the prices, and the political, social, and economic lives. One can penetrate into the thinking of these historians to discover their preoccupations and concerns.

These chroniclers were simple narrators and eyewitnesses to what they saw and experienced, presenting the facts as they appeared to them and leaving the reader to discover and verify a bygone century in its preoccupations and mode of thinking.

Rufāīl Karāmeh el Himsī describes the society of Lebanon in the eighteenth century, its preoccupations, and its mode of living. He clearly reveals the distinctive tendency especially among the Greek Catholic historians to equate their religious identity with their identity.

DOI: 10.4324/9781003023432-2

6   Chronicle Writing

This is how in *Hawādith Lubnān wa sūryah* he presents his autobiography and his promotion by degrees to the sacerdotal order until 1755 when he was ordained a priest. He informs us about his life, his religious order, and the persecutions he and the other priests had to endure from what he calls "*the schismatic Rum,*" the Ottoman governor and others. He says:

> "*Since I had started writing a historical work before I came from Hims, I continued writing with exactness all that was happening in the monastery and Mt Lebanon, particularly the persecutions which my religious order had to suffer from the enemies of the faith and the others along with what was happening to the Greek Catholic Patriarch, bishops, and prelates. Also, I tried my best to write accurately about what happened in my life, and what I could lay my hands on. At that time the good Kyrillos Tanās, the Rūm Catholic Patriarch, had to endure the schismatic persecution and flee from Damascus. I started my history in 1754.*"[2]

Al Himsi is an eyewitness to the events he is relating and seems at the same time to be relying on other available sources, "*and what my hands could lay on.*" His concerns reflect the intermingling of the politics and intermingling of politics and religion in eighteenth-century Lebanon, for – according to him – the events of human history are subject to divine providence which directs, guides, and controls the deeds of men. This, in fact, is his understanding of history, mainly to consider the events a result of the will of God the Almighty, revealing a linear conception of history, a dominant trend among most of the historians of this period. On the other hand, as a Greek Catholic, he sides with his Church against what he calls the "schismatic Rūm." In 1786, he wrote:

> "*As to Schismatic Rūm, the rancorous and the tiresome, they were satisfied with the damage they caused to the church of God in Hims and Damascus and in driving away its subjects from their homes in all directions through contrivance and vain accusation. Needless to add that in the same year they accused the Catholics of Saydnaya of killing a schismatic Rum priest, which obliged them to pay twenty-nine bags (of money) after being deprived of their homes and treated severely.*"[3]

Karāmeh describes the living conditions in the monasteries particularly in northern Lebanon, the story of Hindiyyah,[4] and the feud of 1777 in Bkirki monastery where six nuns were strangled,[5] among them the daughter of Abi Antūn Badrān. The latter appealed to the Amir of Mount Lebanon, Yūsuf al Shihābī (1770–1789)[6] who directly took hold of this monastery and confiscated its valuable objects.

A religious vein characterizes Karami's writing as he expresses loyalty to his religion and advocates the spreading and teaching of the Christian faith. It is in this perspective that he relates about Ahmad Ibn al Azm's death in 1783. He relates:

"A few days later, al Basha died with poison as it was said God had precipitated his death because of his oppression of the Christians and his bad intentions towards them. This is why many of them had to flee to Mount Lebanon, Beirut, and Saida."[7]

A pious tone covers, directs, and dictates Karameh's writing. As a Greek Catholic, he defends his sect against the Rum, and as a Christian he is proud of his faith and is willing to propagate it among the other sects.

As has already been noted, religion and politics are intermingled in Karameh's thinking. He focuses on the history of Lebanon, on the Emirs of the Mountain, the Harafishah family in Baalbek, and on Druze-Christian relations. His interest in neighboring countries – Syria, Palestine, Egypt, or even Europe – are confined within his interest in the history of Lebanon. It is in this outlook that he mentions Muhammad Abu al Dahab,[8] Zaher al 'Umar,[9] and the British Admiral Sidney Smith.

Karameh describes how St. Elias (the Prophet Elijah) appeared to Muhammad Abu al Dahab when he devastated the convent of Mar Elias in Carmel in 1775. He records:

"After few days and on Whit Sunday night, the prophet Elias appeared to him, Sheikh like, and all in white. This unfortunate and unlucky man started screaming and asked for help against this old man (that is Prophet Elias) who as he thought, was trying to kill him. Yet those who were around saw no one. After only two seconds, Abu al Dahab was strangled and died. Subsequently, his soldiers went back to Egypt."[10]

The same event was mentioned by Mikhail Breik,[11] who also attacks Abu al Dahab, affirming that the latter's death was due to his bad intentions toward the Christians.

The two historians – the Greek Catholic and the Rum Orthodox – surpass their secular affiliation to think on a wider level supporting the

Christians against Abu al Dahab. Human history then has a purpose directed toward God who punishes and rewards at the same time.

Karameh describes how al Jazzar besieged Beirut in 1773 and took hold of a French ship which was carrying money to the local merchants and how he bribed the Emir and Mashāyikh of Lebanon. He goes on to relate about the Muscovite arrival in Beirut at the request of Zāher al ᶜUmar, al Jazzar's defeat and his refuge in Zāher al ᶜUmar's territory. Karāmeh gives his opinion blaming Zāher al ᶜUmar for giving refuge to what he names "a deceiver and a traitor" and adds that these events caused Zāher's downfall. Karāmeh is commenting and giving his opinion and is aware of the controversial causes for the fall of Zāher al Umar which were mentioned by other contemporary chroniclers like Abbud al Sabbagh,[12] Mikhail Breik,[13] and others.

Karameh relates about Napoleon Bonaparte's expedition to Egypt and Syria.[14] He is mainly concerned with the repercussion of this expedition on the political situation in Lebanon, but neglects the reasons for this expedition and its cultural and social impact on the whole region. He comments that the Christians were happy for the coming of the French, whereas the Druzes were apprehensive for their arrival in the area: "Bonaparte arrived with his army and besieged the city. The Christians were happy, but the Druzes were frightened."[15] The author seems to be indirectly hinting at the struggle for power and ascendancy between the Druzes and the Christians. When he later describes in detail the meetings and the friendship between the British Admiral Sidney Smith and Emir Bashir Shihab the second of Lebanon,[16] he is most probably drawing the attention to a new kind of European intervention where the great powers protected and patronized the different sects thus playing a major role in the political events of the area.

The local, regional, and European events, the secular, and the religious all intermingle in Karameh's writing, representing different and versatile trends in his historical thinking. He was open to the Christian people overseas and was courageous not to please the Ottoman government or to remain under its protection. In 1768, he wrote about the war between Muscovy and Turkey. This was when the Muscovite emperor defended the Christians against the Sultan who took Christian children instead of the tribute (*al Jizyah*) which was at the time imposed on them. He says:

"*The Russian emperor was moved with zeal towards the Christians. He fought the Islamic countries to deliver these Christians from grief and injustice, as it actually happened.*"[17]

This Christian European trend is also manifested when Karameh relates how in 1787 the Muslims of Damascus prevented the Muscovite and Austrian consuls from staying in their city. The same incident is related by Hanania al Munayyir, a Greek Catholic contemporary of Karameh.[18] The latter adds that the notables of Damascus sent the Consuls a message, saying: "Damascus is the door of al Ka'bah and accepts no consuls in it."[19]

Karameh mentions that in 1787 and during the war between the Ottomans and the Muscovites, Emperor Mikhail advanced with 12,000 soldiers to help the Sultan of the Tartars who was converted to the Christian religion. He relates how the Ottoman Sultan confronted him with 70,000 soldiers and how Catherine the Great precipitated to help her son Mikhail against the Ottomans. Karameh adds:

> "They killed all of them and none of the seventy thousand was saved, and there was an agreement between the king of the Muscovites and the king of Austria to fight the Ottomans."[20]

Karameh shows his sympathy toward the Tartar Sultan who was converted to the Christian faith, and he is at the same time courageous to side with the Christians against the Sultan. This religious trend was accompanied with a sense of belonging to Lebanon and allegiance to the place he was living in. When he later relates how al Jazzar was enraged in 1800 to see the leaders of Mount Lebanon rallying around Bashir II, he is no doubt indicating the importance of unity to build Lebanon on firm grounds.[21]

Karameh relates the events in chronological order, but he is also selective in his choice of these events and bold enough in presenting his thought. This fragile combination between the traditional and the modern induces us to classify him as a chronicler who paves the way into what is called neo-chronicle writing.

Karameh's thinking can be imagined to be departing from a circle composed of three parts: an outward part of the periphery including politics, a middle part representing religion, and a third part, the axis of the circle, the sect which the historian belongs to.

Politics at the periphery is the Ottoman Sultanate, disregarded by the author, yet is able at any moment to penetrate into the other parts of the circle and disrupt its balance.

The second part is religion, Christianity, a very important point of departure for the author and forms a major concept in his understanding of history.

The axis of the circle representing the sect is the core of the historian's thinking. There, we see Karameh retreating in his cell defending the Greek Catholics against what he calls the Schismatic Rum and others. In this sense, the circle which enlarges and decreases in size depending upon the prevalent events and circumstances represents a vivid description of the time of the historian where politics and religion dictate the events, and where the historian, despite his wanderings at times outside his axis to the other parts of the circle, or even outside the circle itself, to talk about the European countries, he at the end returns to the axis of the circle, to his sect, where he finds security, peace, and a feeling of identity.

This trend is prevalent among most of the historians of that period and later periods as well in the history of Lebanon.

1.2 Antonios Abu Khattar al Aynturini (d. 1821)

The second chronicler is Antonios Abu Khattar al Aynturini, a lay Maronite who chronicled the happenings of the nineteenth century on Mount Lebanon giving the Maronites a special status and a role in the sequence of events. Al Aynturini was a hereditary sheikh presiding over the village of 'Aynturini in Jibbat Bsharri. In the last decade of his life, he rose to political prominence in his region and participated in the revolt of the Maronites against Bashir II. With the failure of that revolt, he was captured and tortured and died soon after 1821.[22]

Al Aynturini relied on various sources including the Bible, Ibn al Ibri, Yusifus (Josephus), and others, but he mainly depended on Estephan al Duwayhi.[23] His book *Mukhtasar Tarikh Jabal Lubnan* is the history of a certain district with its special geographic features – the mountain, including extensions to the coast and the interior. It does not, however, reveal an understanding of the Lebanese entity and whether the latter is confined solely to the mountain or extends to the coast and the interior with distinct mountainous characteristics.

There were historical circumstances, in fact, which gave the mountain of Lebanon throughout the period of the Emirate a distinct history. Al Aynturini reveals an awareness, understanding, and assertion of this reality, giving it a clear identity with universal dimensions beyond the confines of the sect while assigning to the Maronites a distinctive role in this reality.

It is worth mentioning that in spite of the author's awareness of the innovations in historical writing in the West – mainly through the graduates of the Maronite School in Rome – he still, while relating the history of Lebanon, moves from one subject to another presenting his concerns while going backward and forward from one century to the next, regressing backward at times without any logical sequence.

Chronicle Writing 11

This is how he moves from the history of Adam and the Old Testament to the New Testament and the mystery of Salvation through Jesus Christ, jumping to the history of cities and then to the Islamic era, the history of Timurlang, the history of notables in Lebanon, and to the events of the eighteenth and the nineteenth centuries. He then goes back to the history of the Crusades and the beginning of Maronite history.

The purpose of al Aynturini is to summarize the events that he read in the various books and to give the reader an idea about the history of Lebanon, adding his own observations as an eyewitness to the events he is relating. In fact, it seems that the author's purpose is to acquaint the Lebanese with their history and the developments that occurred in Lebanon at the end of the eighteenth and the beginning of the nineteenth century when the idea of a Lebanese entity started to take shape having its nucleus in the mountain and the Lebanese Emirate.

Mukhtasar Tarikh Jabal Lubnan can be divided into four axes:

1. A historical survey since the time of Adam till the nineteenth century containing unrelated different subjects.
2. A history of noble families in Lebanon.
3. A history of the Maronites concentrating on the history of Bsharri.
4. Diverse histories at the end of the book on catastrophes, miracles, and oddities.

Our concern here is mainly on the history of the noble families and the Maronites where al Aynturini focuses on the influential families in the history of Lebanon like Banu Shihab, Banu Assaf, Alameddine, Areslan, Hamadeh, and others. He goes back to the ancestor of each family, his coming to Lebanon, his achievements, and his role in the history of the area. This is how he mentions the Shihabi family and their arrival in Lebanon with the Muslim Conquest, their settlement in Syria, and their rule in Lebanon after the end of the Maan family. He enumerates the different Shihabi rulers till he comes to Emir Haidar, the battle of Ain Dara, and the victory over the Alameddine family.

Al Aynturini chronicles the events without mentioning their significance. When he describes the battle of Ain Dara in 1711, for example, he fails to enumerate the repercussions of that battle in the mountain and the consequences that occurred in the political setup of Lebanon when the Druze lost their power and the Maronites prevailed in the mountain. This will no doubt create tension in the history of Lebanon and will engender later drastic circumstances in the history of the mountain. Reaching Emir Bashir al Shihabi, al Aynturini comments expressing his preferences and affiliations. He says:

> "His excellency Prince Bashir ruled Dayr al Qamar, Jbeil, and its vicinities with justice and clemency, and he practiced just law on the high and low. No ruler before him was as just, not accepting a bribe or siding with any one against the other, always listening personally to his people's concerns. He is truly the king of justice. We ask God to keep him ruler for the sake of his people. He is truly the king of justice. We ask God to keep him ruler for the sake of his people. He is truly the king of justice. We ask God to keep him ruler for the sake of his people. He is the prince of this century and era. God keep him till the end of times."[24]

Coming to Banu Assaf and Banu Sayfa, he mentions the Islamic Conquest and the devastation of Kisrawan. To protect the sea coasts from the French Crusaders, the governor of Damascus sent Kurds and Turks who inhabited Tripoli and several coasts in Kisrawan. Among them was a skillful man named Assaf who dwelled in Ghazir and built a citadel and a mosque. His grandson bestowed the government of Jbeil and Batroun on the Hamadeh Shii family.

This is how al Aynturini reaches the Hamadeh family and goes in detail to describe their oppressive rule and the revolt of the population against them. The Ottoman governor waged war against them and followed them to Baalbek, terminating those who remained alive and leaving others to freeze in the snow. Those who remained lived in a very quiet manner in Jbeil deprived of any influence or might. In 1763, Emir Yusuf put an end to their role and power.

Al Aynturini, while chronicling what he considered the main historical events in Lebanon, conveyed a clear picture of the important happenings of the times, reflecting a genre of historical writing where the past is linked to the present and the present to the past. Al Aynturini at the same time seemed to believe in a Lebanon not only in the mountain, but also on a broader level while mentioning the families that were prevalent in the history of Lebanon. In his description, he portrays a picture of a Lebanon that goes beyond the mountain to the south, the north, and the Biqa. It is a Lebanon on the road of proving itself as an entity not confined solely to the mountain, but open to new boundaries in the process of developing into a country of its own. In describing the important families that shaped the history of Lebanon, al Aynturini seems to be conveying a certain perception of historical thinking: the history of a country is based on the history of its inhabitants and their struggle to survive.

Coming to the Maronites, al Aynturini expresses not only his pride in being a Maronite, but he also affirms the continuous loyalty of the Maronite Church to the Roman Church, and to the monastic order of Saint Anthony the Great. He relates how each convent was independent of the other with its special superior until God desired to unite these convents by calling from Aleppo three Maronite God-fearing persons: the first Jibrail Hawwa, the second Abd al Ahad (Abd Allah) Quarali, and the third Yusuf Ibn Batn. They innovated the monastic rules ordained by the holy fathers: obedience, chastity, and humility. This is how they came from Aleppo in February 1694, first to Dayr Qannubin where the Patriarch celebrated mass. There the monks dwelt and the mystical way of life took shape. These solitary monks following the order of Great St Anthony were the basis for the true religious life among the Maronites of Qannubin.

1.3 Haydar Ibn Rida al Rukayni[25] (1711–1784)

While still in the realm of the chroniclers, it is worth mentioning another form of historical thinking confined to a specific locality or a region that bestows identity on its holders and a peculiar sense of belonging. These historians were mostly craftsmen, workers, barbers, farmers, or soldiers. They used colloquial language and some wrote diaries or memoirs to relate the events.

Haydar Ibn Rida al Rukayni is a representative of this kind of popular writing who departed from his locality to address the people and act as a liaison between the educated classes and the rest of the population. He was among those who transmitted the political, social, and economic events giving a vivid picture of the common people's way of life at that time, their customs, values, tastes, and actions. He was among those historians who were able to make people aware of the meaning of history and to write about popular history, giving a picture of the mentality of this strata in the society, their daily preoccupations, the prevalent situation in the mosques, and the places of entertainment and the news that circulated and entertained them at the same time. One can realize that the writings of al Rukayni bear an important meaning that goes beyond simple and innocent appearances to a more profound dimension, and that understanding a society is not confined to what the rulers or the renowned people performed, but in frequenting the streets and the different vicinities and getting introduced to the lives of the common people. This fact was often neglected by the classical historians who as a result failed in understanding the link between literature and art on the one side, and the markets and their inhabitants on the other.

This is how to understand Lebanese historical thinking in its various aspects: one has to delve into the world of the regional historians, understand their attachment to their locality, source of identity, honor, and their reason of existence.

These historians did not confine themselves to power and politics and were not concerned solely with the rulers or high society. They established, on the contrary, a link between the upper classes and the lower strata in society, informing people about the various social and political situations and bringing the events of history to popular understanding, thus providing information to all levels of society.[26]

This is how Haydar Ibn Rida al Rukayni in his book *Jabal Amel fi Qarn*[27] records the political, economic, and social events in Jabal 'Amel from 1749 till 1821. He represents chronicle writing in his method of moving from one subject to the other without any logical sequence or connection between the subjects related. Al Rukayni died before finishing his book, but it was completed by his son.

Al Rukayni focuses on the feudal families who ruled at that time and their relationship with the governor of Saida and the rulers of the neighboring regions.[28]

Al Rukayni describes the feudal families' struggle for power. He described the feud prevalent then among these families while alluding to their cooperation and unity at times when the circumstances demanded that they fight against the governor.

The feudal families then struggled for power and, at times when it was to their benefit, rallied against the governor to protect themselves. In 1759, for example, these families defended themselves in front of the governor of Saida Saad al Din Pasha al 'Azm, who attacked Bilad Bishara, killed people, and ransacked properties. This struggle between the feudal families and the governor was a regular phenomenon in the different regions causing disasters and enormous suffering among the population.

Al Rukayni mentions Zaher al 'Umar, wali' of Acre, and his ambition to dominate the people of Jabal 'Amel. He relates that al Sheikh Nassif and Sheikh Abbas together with the Druses attacked Wadi al Mi'zamieh and defeated Zaher al 'Umar. The latter retaliated, killed many people, and committed atrocities. At other times, however, the relationship between the feudal families and Zaher al 'Umar was peaceful.[29]

Al Rukayni also describes the economic situation, giving an ample idea about prices and the concerns of the lower strata of society and their daily immediate needs without neglecting the calamities of nature and their repercussions, especially on the common people and their way of life.

Al Rukayni bypassed the news about pilgrimages or what occurred in the Ottoman Empire and its various cities. He concentrated on the news of Jabal 'Amel and its adjacent regions, showing a sense of belonging to a certain locality and an affiliation to a specific group.

Al Rukayni gave a panorama of a regional society in Lebanon. He narrated and described the various events in Jabal 'Amel. It was not his aim to think of causes and consequences or to analyze the various aspects in society. He was describing Jabal 'Amel at a time when other historians were preoccupied with the broad political structure in society and what related to the Ottoman Empire.

Al Rukayni provides an example of Lebanese thinking in the eighteenth century who in his description of a specific locality reflects a sense of regionalism which would thrive later to become a potent factor in Lebanese structure. Al Rukayni, a Shi'ite, writing on Jabal 'Amel, gives a picture of the life of the ordinary people introducing us to a society neglected by other historians in the eighteenth century. At the same time, he represents those minorities not dissolved in the ocean of the Ottoman Empire to reflect a kind of a specific regional tendency that will develop and thrive later to form an important element in Lebanese society.

1.4 Concluding Remarks

Chronicle writing reveals the daily lives of the people while describing the economic, social, and political situation in the eighteenth century. The chroniclers installed something of their own factuality and details enabling the readers to assess the different information and draw a picture of a past century in its positive and negative aspects. While it is true that some like Rufail Karameh al Himsi and al Aynturini expressed their point of view in their belief in an entity called Lebanon, tried to understand the significance of current events, and trespassed the confines of Lebanon to mention European countries, still both concentrated on relating the events as they occurred without delving except rarely into causes and consequences. As for al Rukayni, though the idea of a region that he belonged to was prevalent in his writing, still it was confined to relating the events without delving into causes and effects. In this sense, it gave a picture of society at that time and the political situation that prevailed without penetrating into the deeper significance of the various events or analyzing the local and regional circumstances that ensued.

Chronicle writing would develop into a new form in understanding events. Those events would be viewed in their deeper meanings and new conclusions will emerge. A novel view of society would develop where historians would find meaning in various information, reaching conclusions that would enable them not only to understand, but also to analyze and delve into causes and effects. These are the neo-chroniclers, the new group of historians who would approach their subject by giving the information while analyzing and reaching conclusions. This would eventually lead to a better understanding of eighteenth-century society and would help in forming a vision to enlighten the minds and understand the period in a new scope. Hanania al Munayyir and others emerge here as the neo-chroniclers and analytical historians at the same time.

Acknowledgments

Parts of this chapter were originally published as "Rufail Karameh al Himsi (1730–1800) and His Hawadith Lubnan wa Suriya," *Parole de L'Orient* 27 (2002): 133–146.

Notes

1 See: Franz Rozenthal, *A History of Muslim Historiography* (Leiden: E.J. Brill, 1968), 71–86. Also, Tarif Khalidi, *Arabic Historical Thought in the Classical Period* (Cambridge: Cambridge University Press, 1994), 80.
2 Karameh, Rufail al Himsi, *Hawadith Lubnan wa Suryah min sanat 1745–1800*, ed. by Basilius Qattan (Beirut: Jarrous Press, 1984), 7. The translation is mine.
3 Karāmeh, *Hawādith*, 102 (translation mine).
4 Superior of the monastery of Qalb Yasu' in Bkirkī, who pretended to be a saint for several years. See also, Hanānia al Munayyir, *Al Durr al Marsūf fī Tārīkh al Shūf* (Beirut, 1984), 66.
5 The Patriarch took over the monastery and made it his residence, thus becoming the patriarchal seat of the Maronite community. See Karameh, *Hawadith*, 57–58. On the relation of this incident with Hindiyya, see Hanānia al Munayyir, *Al Durr al Marsuf fi Hawadit al Shuf* (Beirut, 1984), 66.
6 On Yusuf al Shihabi, see Kamal Salibi, *The Modern History of Lebanon* (New York, NY: Caravan Books, 1993), 14, 16–17, and 20.
7 Karameh, *Hawadith*, 78.
8 A Mamluk Emir and regent of Ottoman Egypt (1735–1750).
9 On Zaher al 'Umar and al Jazzar (died 1804), see Amnon Cohen, *Palestine in the 18th Century: Patterns of Government Administration* (Jerusalem: Magners Press, 1973), 311–328.
10 Karameh, *Hawadith*, 47.
11 Greek Orthodox historian in eighteenth-century Bilād al Shām.
12 Discussed in chapter 3 of this study.

13 See Mikhail Briek, *Tarikh al Sham* (Harisa: Matbaat al Qiddis Boulos, 1930), 104.
14 Karameh, *Hawadith*, 157.
15 Karameh, *Hawadith*, 157.
16 See on this subject Kamal Salibi, *The Modern History of Lebanon*, 21.
17 Karameh, *Hawadith*, 36.
18 See chapter 2 in this study.
19 Karameh, *Hawadith*, 9.
20 Karameh, *Hawadith*, 103.
21 See Karameh, *Hawadith*, 169.
22 Yusuf al Dibs, Tarikh Suriah (Beirut: al Matbat al Umumiah al Maruniah, 1907).
23 On the Maronite historians, see Kamal Salibi, *Maronite Historians of Mediaeval Lebanon* (Beirut: American University, 1959).
24 Abi Khattar al Aynturini, *Mukhtasar Tarikh Jabal Lubnan*, ed. by Ilyas Qattar (Beirut: Dar Lahd Khater, 1983), 54.
25 The only information we have on this author is what he mentioned in his book *Jabal Amel fi Qarn*, ed. by Muhammad Huteit (Beirut: Dar al fikr al Lubnani, 1996) that he was 43 in 1735. See also: Muhammad Kazem Makki, *Al Haraka al Adabiah fi Jabal Amel* (1963); Usama Anuti, *Al Haraka al Adabiah fi Bilad al Sham fi al Qarn al Thamin ashar* (Beirut: al Maktaba al Sharquiyah, 1971), 208.
26 On popular history, see: Abraham Marcus, *The Middle East on The Eve of Modernity: Aleppo in the Eighteenth Century* (New York, NY: Columbia University Press, 1989), 219–237; Tarif Khaldi, *Arabic Historical Thought in the Classical Period*, 292; Jack Crabbs, *The Writing of History in Nineteenth Century Egypt: A Study in National Transformation* (Cairo: The American University of Cairo Press, 1984), 38–39; Alan Swingewood, *The Myth of Mass Culture* (London: MacMillan, 1977), 2, 4, 10, and 16.
27 Jabal Amel is in South Lebanon and features hills extending from the southern Litani River to the Palestinian border.
28 For further information on the political situation in Jabal Amel, see Stefan Winter, *The Shiites of Lebanon Under Ottoman Rule 1516–1788* (Cambridge: Cambridge University Press, 2010), 117–145. Chapter 5 which focuses on the Shiite community vis-a-vis the Shihabi Emirate in the new context of decentralized rule in the eighteenth century.
29 See Ahmad Huteit, *Jabal 'Amel*, 100.

Reference List

Al Aynturini, Abi Khattar. *Mukhtasar Tarikh Jabal Lubnan*, ed. by Ilyas Qattar. Beirut: Dar Lahd Khater, 1983.
Al Dibs, Yusuf. *Tarikh Suriah*. Beirut: al Matbat al Umumiah al Maruniah, 1907.
Al Munayyir, Hanānia. *Al Durr al Marsūf fī Tārīkh al Shūf*. Beirut, 1984.
Anuti, Usama. *Al Haraka al Adabiah fi Bilad al Sham Khilal al Qarn al Thamin Ashar*. Beirut: al Maktabat al Sharqiah, 1971.

Briek, Mikhail. *Tarikh al Sham*. Harissa: Matbaat al Qiddis Boulos, 1930.

Cohen, Amnon. *Palestine in the 18th Century: Patterns of Government Administration*. Jerusalem: Magners Press, 1973.

Crabbs, Jack. *The Writing of History in Nineteenth Century Egypt: A Study in National Transformation*. Cairo: The American University of Cairo Press, 1984.

Huteit, Muhammad, ed. *Jabal Amel fi Qarn*. Beirut: Dar al fikr al Lubnani, 1996.

Karameh, Rufail al Himsi. *Hawadith Lubnan wa Suryah min sanat 1745–1800*, ed. by Basilius Qattan. Beirut: Jarrous Press, 1984.

Khalidi, Tarif. *Arabic Historical Thought in the Classical Period*. Cambridge: Cambridge University Press, 1994.

Makki, Muhammad Kazem. *Al Haraka al Adabiah fi Jabal Amel*. Beirut: Dar al Andalus, 1963.

Marcus, Abraham. *The Middle East on The Eve of Modernity: Aleppo in the Eighteenth Century*. New York, NY: Columbia University Press, 1989.

Rozenthal, Franz. *A History of Muslim Historiography*. Leiden: E.J. Brill, 1968.

Salibi, Kamal. *Maronite Historians of Mediaeval Lebanon*. Beirut: American University, 1959.

———. *The Modern History of Lebanon*. New York, NY: Caravan Books, 1993.

Swingewood, Alan. *The Myth of Mass Culture*. London: MacMillan, 1977.

Winter, Stefan. *The Shiites of Lebanon Under Ottoman Rule 1516–1788*. Cambridge: Cambridge University Press, 2010.

2 Neo-Chroniclers

2.1 Hanania al Munayyir (1756–1823)

We move to a Greek Catholic historian, the priest Hanania al Munayyir, a chronicler, a neo-chronicler, and an analytical historian whose book *al Durr al Marsuf fi Hawadith al Shuf* ("The Paved Treasures in the Events of al Shuf"[1]) relates the story of the Shihabi Emirate in Lebanon from the year 1697 to 1807. As a chronicler, al Munayyir followed the yearly sequence in relating the events. As a neo-chronicler, he not only registered the events within the chronological framework of their original occurrence, but while narrating, he also revealed the events as possessing a structure, an order of meaning interpreting and giving his opinion when fit. As an analytical historian, al Munayyir approached the events in a thematic way showing his versatility and his understanding of the history of Mount Lebanon in the context of regional and international history, reflecting an original trend in Lebanese historical thinking in the eighteenth century.

Al Munayyir belongs to a group of literary men who gathered around Bashir II (1788–1840) and for whom the writing of history was only one aspect of multiple literary activities. They not only produced the histories of their age, but were also the fathers of the poetic and linguistic movement of nineteenth-century Lebanon.[2]

As an eyewitness, al Munayyir was able to be aware of the factors that were to constantly disturb the structure of the Lebanese entity. He was therefore prepared to form a vision of an autonomous, but fragile, Lebanon, which would continually be subject to local, regional, and international influences, disturbing its peace and shaking its reason of existence. Al Munayyir was among other Christian historians who were able to acquire well-grounded education in the fields of philosophy, polemics, historiography, and philology. Those men as mentioned

DOI: 10.4324/9781003023432-3

before were precursors of the famous Arab literary and intellectual renaissance of the nineteenth century.[3]

Al Munayyir asserts that his writing involves the recent history of his time and that he uses verified sources to support his claims. At the same time, he links the past with the present and the future. In so doing, he demonstrates an objective trend by asking future generations to improve the content whenever necessary or continue in the same endeavor for the glory of God.

Al Munayyir chronicles the events in their yearly sequence, focusing on the political affairs of the Imara (Emirate) and its ruling houses in whose orbit everything else revolves. He mentions the prominent families following their importance in society.[4] He is aware that the period he is discussing is a formative period in the history of Lebanon and is worth reflecting upon. Al Munayyir's scope widens as he looks at an entity called Lebanon and not only at a specific prince or religious community. He therefore extends his research and commentary to involve the Lebanese community with its own local tradition, which he affirms should be preserved.

Al Munayyir's account of the political situation reflects the struggle for power in the Emirate which opened doors before the external intrusion of outside forces in the affairs of Lebanon. He introduces us to the society as he relates the struggle between the Qaysi Yamani and the Yazbaki Jumblati, which, in his opinion, constitutes a basis and prelude to religious and sectarian conflict between the different sects during that time. This eventuality allowed a split in the edifice of the Emirate and prepared it for an evolution toward a political entity that carried with it the vicious remnants of past problems and conflicts.[5]

Writing in the eighteenth century, al Munayyir was not completely aware either of the importance of the Battle of Ayn Dara between the Qaysi and the Yamani as a turning point in the history of the Emirate or the repercussions that were to ensue as a result for the future of Lebanon. Viewed from a later date, however, the ascendancy of the Druzes, which until then had been prominent in the mountain, soon began to fade. The expulsion of the Yamanites reaped drastic consequences in decreasing the number of the Druzes and increasing the numerical strength of the Maronites.[6]

Al Munayyir is content to describe Haidar Shihab's power and his skill in taking advantage of the feud between the feudal families and plays on this conflict to achieve his goal in paying the arrear taxes. The Emir, ruling from 1730 to 1735, was able to instigate intrigues among those notables to prevail and gain support himself.[7] Al Munayyir moves further in his style of narrating events, to explain, reflect, and give his opinion on the various issues taking place, either directly or by insinuation. One can say he was endeavoring to write what Gaston White calls "proper history."[8]

This is how al Munayyir describes the Yazbaki Junblati struggle[9] stressing the theme of the struggle for power, searching for the cause and the significance of the events, as well as discussing Ottoman rule and its dangers on the security of the country. He explains how the Ottomans kept their control over the Emirate, electing and changing governors, imposing taxes, and trying to take advantage of the Lebanese situation in order to bring about the fall of the competing factions, thus following a policy of "divide to control."

This Ottoman interference in the affair of Lebanon according to al Munayyir reached its climax during the rule of al Jazzar. Here, he extends his interest to other areas such as Palestine and Egypt, insinuating the reality without which understanding of the events occurring would not be possible if devoid of its local, regional, and international context. Such a period, no doubt, propagates a continuity from a previous order carrying with it the seeds which would thrive to grow later on fertile ground, to blossom and to interact with new elements that would lay the basis for a new chapter in the history of Lebanon.

Al Munayyir is aware of Lebanon's vulnerability becoming acute when the Russian squadron was sent to Beirut by Daher al Umar. The chronicler and the neo-chronicler join here as al Munayyir relates minutely the events and comments on the sound of canons reaching Damascus for four consecutive days without affecting the city's sandy stones, or when describing the siege and the suffering of those people who were forced to eat donkey meat to sustain themselves. Al Munayyir is the storyteller, the observer, the reporter, and the preacher who advises people to draw lessons from the events. This didactic tone continues as he relates how al Jazzar held Bashir's destiny in his hands and with him the whole Emirate. We witness here a complete picture not only of al Jazzar's power but also of the vulnerability of Lebanon caught between internal tension and external exploitation.

Al Munayyir places the history of Lebanon in its international context as he describes Napoleon Bonaparte's arrival at Acre in 1799. He expresses the positive attitude of the Christians and was aware that the tension would intensify among the people: those who support the Europeans and those who consider them as Kukffar.[10]

The European intervention furthered the tension between al Jazzar and Bashir II when the latter refused to join the governor against the French, and to join Sidney Smith, the British general. In recounting how Smith wrote to the Ottoman authorities describing al Jazzar's oppressiveness and warning them of future additional misunderstanding between the two countries,[11] al Munayyir is not only the observer following the sequence of events, but also an actor on the stage and a partisan of Bashir and Smith against al Jazzar.

Al Munayyir recounts how Emir Bashir started to consolidate his rule by curbing the power of the feudal families and profiting from the prevalent religious circumstances to become the sole authoritative master in Lebanon following a policy of divide to control. Al Munayyir is now the analytical historian who penetrates the meaning of the events and sees beyond the façade to draw lessons and visualize a vision of a Lebanon whose future would continue to be exploited by regional and international powers and involved in matters beyond its control. Bashir was able to fully control Mount Lebanon for 52 years, but his entanglement in foreign affairs added to the weakness of his internal structure, leading to the collapse of the Emirate. A new organization for Lebanon was to come forth, one which would carry with it the germs, which at any moment could infect the body of the whole edifice and throw it asunder.[12]

Al Munayyir's thought comes to the fore here as an analytical historian who searches into the causes and significance of events, drawing conclusions and wisdom for future generations to follow. This is how his religious tendencies are manifested in his theistic approach, putting his writing in the realm of linear history where the events are directed toward eternity. In this way, one can learn from the righteous and evade the path of the sinful.

What is significant in al Munayyir's writing is the attention to the importance of the separation between church and state, a secular trend reflecting the openness of the Christian historians to the new ideas coming from Europe. This secular trend is manifested when al Munayyir does not confine himself to relating the story of his own community, and also in placing the history of the Greek Catholics in the context of the history of Lebanon as a whole. This does not contradict his philosophy of history when he considers the events as leading to a purpose beyond the realm of the visible universe. Al Munayyir's liberal and modern ideas in his attitude toward women are also evident when, for example, he declared that 'Ali Daher did not allow his daughters to marry so as not to put them under a man's control.[13]

The author's inclination to express his opinion or present an interpretation of his own is demonstrated throughout his book. Writing in 1777, he does not shy away from calling the nun Hindiyya[14] a liar and crooked and, fearing that the reader will accuse him of superficiality or bias, he refers him/her to his book *The History of the Religious Orders* where details and answers to his accusations are made available.[15] Before that time, in 1775, when Ibrahim al Sabbagh, Daher al 'Umar's assistant, was hanged, he comments, "This is a warning for all stingy people."[16] When he relates the attack on Hijaz by 'Ali al Kabir in 1769, he provides the apparent purpose of the attack: to overthrow the Sharif of Mecca, and then Ali's hidden goal: to subdue the whole area.[17] When, alas, Abu'l Dahab persecuted the Christians and destroyed the Convent of Mar Elias in el Karmel, al Munayyir does not hesitate to point out God's wrath which would be brought down on Earth as a result of such acts. On his death bed, Abu'l Dahab had a nightmare of an old man trying to kill him. Al Munayyir sees in this a punishment for Abu'l Dahab's hatred of the Christians. He writes: *"His spirit gone, he died and went to hell, what a wretched death."*[18]

This vogue of commenting, voicing his opinions and analysis, is not confined to political events. It is part of al Munayyir's style in being not merely an observer, but a crucial actor on stage. In 1781, he was among those priests imprisoned by the governor of Bekaa for one day because they went fishing.[19] In 1792, he was present when the Damascene soldiers attacked Zahleh.[20] In 1804, he declared his satisfaction with the death of al-Jazzar composing poems on the occasion.[21] This involvement, however, is mostly manifested, as we have seen before, when he digresses from his political or religious occupation, either to give a history of a locality a kind of flashback or to concentrate on the affairs of daily life.

In 1772, while he was discussing Abu'l Dahab's seizure of Beirut, he alludes to the importance of the city and relates its history going back to the times when it was under Christian rule, then Muslim rule. He relates how the king of Venice destroyed the city when his son was killed in an ambush.[22] He adds that the city was rebuilt by the Ma'n and then the Shihabis.[23] Al Munayyir even provides considerable information revealing the conditions behind the founding of what later came to be known as Dayr al-Qamar. Above the forest facing B'akline where the Tannukhs used to rule was a devastated convent, which the Christians were unable to restore.[24] They used to gather at night under the moonlight, to make up for the lost hours of the day. Later, the place came to be called the convent of the moon, Dayr al-Qamar. Al Munayyir also notes that "Banu Ma'n later lived there."[25] Tannus al-Shidyak adds that that there was a picture in the form of a moon carved on a rock on the wall of what was called the Church of the Hill (*Kanisat al-tallah*).[26]

The author's involvement in religious events does not prevent him from dwelling on the affairs of daily life, showing his ability and wit in adding a spark to the routine of political and military tensions. In 1756, he recounts how the Arabs robbed a pilgrimage and cooked pearls thinking it was rice.[27] In 1792, speaking of high prices and famine, he recounts the story of a man who tried to eat his daughter, but was not able to slaughter her. He then went to one of his neighbors where he ate preserved meat and died. Al Munayyir's wit is manifested here as he exclaims: "Afraid to die from starvation, he died from saturation."[28]

Al Munayyir reflected Lebanese thinking and preoccupations in the eighteenth century. Commenting in general on Lebanese historians, Dr. Ahmad Beydoun in his book *Identité Confessionnelle et Temps Sociale Chez les Historiens Libanais Contemporains* observes, "Le Liban des historiens s'allonge ou se rétrécit non seulement suivant la période considérée, mais aussi suivant les appartenances diverses des auteurs."[29] ("The Lebanon of the historians expands or shrinks not only depending on the period of time considered, but also following the diverse affiliations of its authors").

To what extent can Beydoun's statement be applied to al Munayyir's writing? Did al Munayyir really present the events according to his Christian or Greek Catholic affiliations or did he try to present the events as they happened without bias or preconceived ideas? Al Munayyir lived in a political structure in Lebanon where the ruler was striving to preserve his autonomy against external encroachment and the ambitions of the notable families who were struggling for power. Druzes and Christians were competing for lands and political influence, the Ottomans were striving to preserve their control, and the European powers were profiting from the situation commercially, politically, and ideologically to penetrate the area defending one sect against the other to help in augmenting the religious tension and await the slightest occasion to bring this tension to their service with ease and vehemence. Hanania al Munayyir, with other Christian historians around Bashir II, was aware, so it seems, of the internal and external political situation of that period and was, at the same time, conscious of the importance and uniqueness of Lebanon. They, as a result, produced a "secular" and political history focusing on the struggle for political power, trying not merely to describe, but also to explain and give messages, hinting to the importance of harmony and agreement in maintaining the state. Al Munayyir, in his description, tries to present the events truthfully because he considers those events as paved treasures (*Durr Marsuf*) to be preserved in the memory as didactic experiences in the future. In this way, the events of the past are not mere spectacles to be observed or related, but are activities of thought and experiences to reflect upon and learn from to set a better future. One can truly say in this context that "history writing and historical consciousness are not spheres of praxis that are simply determined in terms of the past; they are present activities aimed essentially at posterity. The inherited text or thing does not solely belong to the origin from which it emerged, but in its original character as what presences with us, it is also destined communicatively towards us by virtue of being in our world."[30]

It is here that al Munayyir appears as a man of his age and of future ages as well. His historical thinking stands at a crossroad between the eighteenth and the nineteenth centuries. As a historian, he was able to combine the old and the new: The chronicler who relates the events in its yearly sequence, the neo-chronicler who delves into the meaning of the events, and the analytical historian who rethinks the meaning of his data, interprets, gives his opinion, and predicts consequences for the various events. Al Munayyir was not only the theistic "eschatological" historian who views the events of history as leading to a definite purpose beyond the visible world but also the heuristic and innovative historian who was able to rid himself of the confines of his religious community and think on a wider scale to explore new horizons, penetrate new spaces, and examine several subjects – economic, political, social, and genealogical – and provide details to inform, warn, edify, and entertain.

Al Munayyir was able, based on the events he was witnessing, to understand Lebanon as a unique reality, an entity and a community with a continuous historical tradition. This entity, as he viewed it, was fragile and torn between internal, regional, and international tendencies. Aware of the importance of the period he was witnessing as a basis for the understanding of later events in modern Lebanon, Al Munayyir draws a panoramic picture not only of the political struggle evident during that time, or of the family feuds, but also of the social and other factors that would later develop to form what may be regarded as a country unique of its kind in the Arab world. He observed with sadness, however, that this entity was suffering from internal struggle and inviting foreign interference in its affairs. He predicted the outcome to make him form a vision of a turbulent, agitated, and restless future that will continue to trigger this unique entity.

Al Munayyir describes the Christian mountain as having strong relations with the West and a Druze mountain with Christians living in its midst and enjoying social and religious liberties. He also describes the Beirut harbor alongside a mountain inhabited by Druzes, Christians, and Muslims as well. On the other hand, he talks about the Christian missionaries opening schools in different localities, as well as their role as advisors to the rulers which he stressed as one not to be ignored. It also seems rather intrinsic not to forget the thriving silk produce which maintained an economic relation with Europe and made Beirut not only a center of trade but also a place of interaction in the area.

Al Munayyir forms a vision through his writings and the exclusive approach with which he handled narrating events. He seems aware that this glowing picture carries within it the seeds of conflict and dissension. Failing to direct their allegiance toward the right cause, the Lebanese might at any moment disrupt this structure and direct its uniqueness toward destruction instead of construction. This is why in 1800, following a struggle between Emir Bashir and the sons of Emir Yusuf, when an agreement was reached whereby Bachir would govern the Druze mountain, and Husayn and his brother Jbeyl (Byblos), al Munayyir comments: *"I do not think this will last for a long time for as usual these people lack integrity and straightforwardness of opinion."*[31] He then quotes a poet – without mentioning his name – who warns people to preserve the heart from grief for like a broken glass, it is always hard to repair what was once broken.[32]

Hanania al Munayyir's thinking shows that history will repeat itself. The struggle for power will remain predominant inviting constant regional and international interference. The laws of history revealing continuity and change will remain in Lebanon, but will not contribute in al Munayyir's vision of stability, security, or comfort to human life. Al Munayyir is analyzing the situation while chronicling the events, opening a screen to the readers to draw meanings from the events, to learn, understand, and reach conclusions.

Al Munayyir is the neo-chronicler who paved the way for analytical history and a broader outlook in fathoming events and understanding them.

2.2 Niqula al Turk (1763–1828)

Discovering the outside world started to become a trend in the eighteenth century where the historians endeavored to go out of the confines of regional events toward other horizons to interact with other cultures, to discover, learn, and be warned. The historians started to look outside their locality, developing a broader conception of history and looking beyond their immediate concerns. Until then, and from about the sixteenth century, the Lebanese historians – mainly Christians – displayed only a limited interest in events taking place in Western Europe. They were, in general, clerics; hence, it is perhaps understandable that they were more concerned by Western Europe's religious influence than its secular impact.

Niqūlā al Turk was the first Lebanese historian with a secular bent to devote a historical work to the events of the French Revolution and to Bonaparte's expedition to Egypt in 1798. Although seemingly unaware of the Enlightenment and the sociopolitical movements that preceded the Revolution, he nonetheless draws attention in his work to the beginning of a new phase in the history of Western influence upon the Arab world which would come to challenge its complacency as well as its sociopolitical life.

Niqūlā ibn Yūsuf ibn Nāsīf Āghā al Turk (1763–1828), a Greek Catholic, was born and laid to rest in Dayr al-Qamar, in Mount Lebanon. His ancestors were Greeks from Constantinople, whence he derived his surname, al Turk. He entered the service of the emir of Lebanon, Bashīr Shihāb II, and was sent to Egypt to observe and report on the French expedition. Al Turk remained there, in Damietta, from 1798 till 1804, while collecting the material necessary for his account of this historical event.[33]

Al Turk admires the European as a warrior and as an administrator describing his presence in the Egyptian society as an encounter between two civilizations and expressing his reflection as a Lebanese historian on this challenge. Here, new questions arise showing a development of thinking as a result of the changes that occurred internationally, the French Revolution and the rise of Napoleon Bonaparte – reflections dealing with the link between the history of Europe and the history of the Middle East, between local history and universal history.

Describing the French fleet that landed in Alexandria, al Turk writes:

> *"And their fleet was constituted of three hundred and eighty vessels having on board thirty thousand soldiers and another twenty-three thousand, including generals, majors, officers, commissaries, secretaries, women, children, and mariners, a total of fifty-three thousand individuals. The commander-in-chief was General Bonaparte, who was thirty years old. He was very daring, always lucky in battles, and was able to conquer Italy, Venice, and other countries."*[34]

Al-Turk gazes in wonder at the superiority and grandeur of the French forces, at the number of French Navy ships and of people on board. He also admires the bravery of their chief, General Bonaparte, as manifested in his military campaigns in Italy and elsewhere. If we try to go beyond al Turk's words, we realize that his admiration of the French military is pregnant with his conviction that the forces arrayed before him are far superior to their local counterparts.

Al Turk describes the difference between the Europeans and Egyptians, reflecting an awareness of a beginning of an encounter between the East and the West. He describes the hostile feelings of the people and their willingness to resist, but adds that there was only one barrel of gunpowder in the citadel of Alexandria, then considered the key to Egypt. This leads him to contrast the Europeans with local soldiers, saying:

> "*The fire power of the French is unbearable and their methods of war are harsh. They possess all of the resources for the art of war, about which the Mamluks and the Arabs have not the slightest idea. The latter are horsemen unable to handle [any arms] except sword and spear, while the French avail themselves of firing weapons in an extraordinary way. They are soldiers of exceptional bravery; their hearts are as solid as rocks. They are not attached to life and do not fear death, but face it with serenity.*"[35]

The European warrior, according to al Turk, is strong, courageous, efficient, resolute, and versed in the sciences. The generals share the attribute of their warriors, but bring to the battlefield greater skills in the sciences and in the art of war.

As an administrator, the French, according to al Turk, is professional. Al Turk evidently admires the various tools introduced by the French to facilitate the administration of Egypt – not merely the technological, such as the printing press, but also the organizational, such as the municipal and general councils. Al Turk draws the attention to Bonaparte's invitation to the sheikhs, 'ulamă', and notables to participate in French-controlled rule and his desire to negotiate with them as the leaders of the Egyptian community, thus insinuating a beginning of national awareness or a kind of indigenous leadership.

Al Turk at the same time presents the European as a skillful politician who tries to understand the nature of the conquered people, appeals to what concerns them most namely, their religious beliefs – and shows readiness to involve them in the persons of their 'ulamă', sheikhs, and notables, in their own government. At the same time, the European is pictured as an obstinate leader adept at using the law to achieve his objectives and willing to resort to force when all else fails. The archetype of this characterization is Bonaparte himself, described by al Turk as "a great hero with formidable energy" whose soldiers loved him "as men love women."[36]

When describing French social life, al Turk also indicates the hostile reaction of the Egyptian people to customs and manners alien to their traditions and way of thinking. But this hostility went much deeper than mere differences in lifestyle, for it was grounded in the religious orientation of Middle Eastern society. It was from this perspective that the Egyptian Muslims equated the *ifranj* with the Christians and, on several occasions, took revenge upon the local Christian community.

According to al Turk, after the arrival of several European consuls in Cairo in 1218/1803 and the implementation of the Capitulations, some Christians responded by dressing in a manner which did not follow the dictates of tradition. For this and other reasons, representatives of the Muslim majority met with the emir banneret, Ibrāhīm Bey, to make the following complaint.

"It is unacceptable that a Muslim country like ours, which is the door to al Ka'ba, be regarded as an ifranj region which allows the Christians to ride horses, wear Islamic clothes, and not abide by local customs."[37]

Here, al Turk not only records his observations, but also justifies the repugnance of Muslims. *"On the other hand, it was very difficult for the ifranj to enter freely into Egyptian society, especially when the Egyptians saw their women unveiled and shamelessly circulating in the streets with the ifranj and dwelling in their houses. The Egyptians could not bear these dreadful scenes."* It was enough to see the wine pubs spread into all of the marketplaces of Cairo, even into some mosques. This spectacle rendered the whole atmosphere to the Muslims and, in each instance, they wished they were dead.[38]

Al Turk offered a panorama of French life in Egyptian society to explain why the latter refused to accept European customs. He says:

"The Egyptians cannot accept a people like this: firstly, because their religion is in opposition to that of the French; secondly, because their language is dissimilar to the French one; thirdly, [because] this is [also] true of their fashions; [and] fourthly, [because] there is an old enmity between the Egyptians and the French". He concludes

that the Egyptians could not accept French rule since it was something *"against nature."*[39]

Al Turk goes further. What he apparently means by this last statement is that a wide gap separated the French from the local population in all areas, whether religion, language, or race. Moreover, Egyptians had always been suspicious of Western ambitions in the Middle East. Although al Turk was a Christian, he shared the Arabic language with the Egyptians, as well as virtually the same traditions. However, he was seemingly able to separate much of his attachment to his own roots from his openness to Western civilization in the picture he paints of the French in Egyptian society.

Despite al Turk's almost total disregard for the intellectual impact of the French expedition, he is nonetheless able to bring to life a dramatic encounter between East and West, the first in a series that would redefine the terms of the challenge posed by the West and the response of the East to it.

Al Turk was on a mission to observe and record. His introduction also tells us that he was writing for the benefit of students of history in the hope that later generations would profit from his chronicle and draw lessons for the future. Perhaps al Turk was aware that he was opening new doors and laying a solid foundation for later historical interpretations and later reflections on the question of Western intrusions and Eastern reactions. In this sense, he was an innovator.

As we have seen, al Turk contrasts European and Muslim Egypt, beginning with European superiority – and Egyptian backwardness – in weaponry and technology. Clearly, he is indicating what he feels to be the key factor in European strength and urging the recognition of this reality upon his readers in the Middle East. The second element to be contrasted is the difference in temperament, mentality, and customs between the two societies. At this point, al Turk is apparently approaching the problem from the Egyptian point of view and exploring the reasons for the hostility of the indigenous population toward French rule. He also draws attention to a very important point, namely, the "unnatural" character of the French occupation. He then presents his own ideas about persons and events.

The idea of national awareness runs through al Turk's *Mudhakkarăt*. The author emphasizes the difference between French and Egyptian customs and language, drawing attention to primary elements of the nationalist sentiment, a theme which later writers will develop and argument.

National loyalty, however, must not obstruct the workings of reason and blind people to the achievements of others. While registering differences between the French and the Egyptians – whether in religion or in their way of life – the author cannot but see the superiority of the former in the fields of science and technology. He also realizes that the French experience is different from anything the Egyptians have ever known before and that it deserves, by its very nature, further thought leading to a reexamination of values.

Lastly, al Turk sees the link between European and Middle Eastern history. His portrayal of the European in Egyptian society, his knowledge of events occurring in Europe, his detailed description of the French occupation, British intervention, Ottoman policy, Mamlŭk resistance and defeat, and, finally, the Egyptian reaction to these events, all imply a move from a narrow view of history, in which closed and confined religious interests preoccupy writers, to a more comprehensive view, in which events taking place in the world are linked and interrelated – a move from local history to universal history.

The European in Niqŭlă al Turk's writing represents a challenge above all else; indeed, his very presence poses many questions. How may a society reconcile closed religious conservatism with open intellectual curiosity? How may it follow the path of Western progress in an authentic manner? How is Lebanon an example and a challenge? In many instances, these are questions with which Middle Eastern societies are still grappling as they face the European West.

2.3 Haidar Ahmad al Shihabi (1761–1835)

The last, but not least chronicler and neo-chronicler that we are dealing with here is Haidar al Shihabi: A prince and a statesman who belonged to the Shihabi family which presided over the affairs of Lebanon on behalf of the Ottoman Sultan between 1697 and 1841. Educated privately in the manner of an Arab prince, he gained the confidence of his relative Emir Bashir II (1789–1840) and became a member of his inner circle. This enabled him to write his history, basing it on official documents that he had access to. He continued chronicling the events till his death.[40]

Al Shihabi gathered around him a group of prominent scholars who worked together such as Tannus and Faris al Shidyak, Butrus Karama, Niqula al Turk, Nasif al Yazigi, and others, but it was Haidar himself who gave the book its final shape. This method of composition explains why the book exists in different forms.

Al Ghurar al Hisan fir Akhbar Abna al Zaman (The most illustrious Aspects of the Narratives of the Times) is divided into three parts, each given a separate title by later copyists, but not by the writer himself. The first part starts with 622 and runs till 1697, the end of the Manid dynasty, the second from 1697 till 1818, and the third from 1819 till 1827. This study will focus on the second and third part, mainly on Lebanon in the eighteenth and beginning of the nineteenth centuries.[41]

Al Shihabi can be considered both a chronicler and a neo-chronicler. As a chronicler, he followed the yearly sequence moving from one subject to the other without any logical continuity. As a neo-chronicler, he explains at times, comments, and gives his opinion at other times. He gives an ample picture of Lebanon under the Emirate reflecting a belief in an entity special in its setup and identity. Living at a crossroads between the eighteenth and the nineteenth centuries, al Shihabi portrays a welcoming land where many nations came and departed leaving their traces to engender an original, versatile, multicultural, and unique country with special characteristics of its own.

Al Shihabi starts the second part with the rule of the Shihabs after the death of Ahmad al Ma'ni in 1697. The *firman* (decree) from the Ottoman Sultan to the governor of Sidon assigned prince Haidar, son of Musa al Shihabi, as the ruler of the district previously under Banu Ma'n.[42] Emir Bashir I would be the interim governor until prince Haidar reached maturity.

Al Shihabi praises Bashir I, describing him as an able ruler, an honorable prince and a noble master. He then shifts directly to relate about a decomposed corpse found in a tomb in one of the vicinities with iron chains around his feet and neck. Departing from there, and to be faithful to the yearly sequence he was following as a chronicler, he mentions the rise of prices followed by the miraculous events of that year – the appearance of a planet with a den in the sky. He concludes that it was a year with miraculous happenings and aridity.

Al Shihabi is preoccupied mainly with the political situation under the Shihabi's and relations with the Ottoman governors. This is how he focuses on Bashir I's support of the governor of Sidon against his enemies – the Shiite Qaysi ben Ali al Saghir in Jabal Amel. The governor gave Emir Bashir the land of Safad as a compensation while the latter propagated his interests in giving privileges to his supporters. Emir Bashir was later poisoned by prince Haidar, who at that time had reached maturity and was able to assume responsibilities. Here, Haidar al Shihabi expresses his admiration for Bashir with these words *"He was a courageous prince, bold and obeyed, generous and handsome. Blonde and tall. He reached his fifties without any successor except his nephew, prince Mansour son of prince Ali. In his days, the Qaysis prevailed and the Yamanis weakened.*"[43]

Haidar al Shihabi praised Emir Haidar as the new prince. He writes: "*The districts of Lebanon acknowledged his rule. Emir Haidar protected his princedom. He was a master to be revered and an heir who bequeathed the inheritance to his descendants.*"[44]

Al Shihabi here is referring to the "district of Lebanon" when the princedom became fully autonomous. Haidar is now the ruler of the north as well as south Lebanon and with a secular authority recognized as legitimate by most of its subjects.

Haidar al Shihabi describes the battles that Emir Haidar waged against the Shi'ites, his ambitions and his skill in adding lands under his control. What draws the attention is the greed of the various governors who bestowed privileges to whomever bribed them with presents and the like.

What is, however, of utmost importance is al Shihabi's description of the Battle of Ayndara in 1711 where the Qaysi faction prevailed and the Yamanis were defeated. This battle was crucial and resulted in changing the structure of these feudal families. The Yamani's defeat resulted in drastic repercussions on the balance of power in Lebanon between the two main communities then, Druzes and the Maronites. It seems that this trend of bypassing the importance of the Battle of Ayndara was prevalent among the historians of the eighteenth century who at the time were preoccupied with the details of the battle and the restructuring of the feudal system. The balance of power between the Druzes and the Maronites was a subject, as we have seen that they neglected.[45]

Haidar Ahmad al Shihabi is the chronicler who relates the events without endeavoring to search for causes and effects. The writer's aim is to give an ample picture of the history of the Emirate aided by the primary resources he had access to and the valuable documents that were within his reach.[46]

Coming to Emir Bashir II, Haidar describes him as a respected prince and a noble young man, powerful and with utmost sagacity and intelligence. He was gentle and loved by the people.[47]

Al Shihabi relates how the reign of Bashir II marked the apex of Shihabi power. He relates how Bashir crushed his enemies inside Lebanon, extended his influence into northern Palestine and the plains of the interior and obtained the right to deal directly with the Ottoman government.

Al Shihabi enumerates the trouble that Emir Bashir encountered from the various feudal families and from Emir Yusuf, the previous emir. Al Jazzar was his ally at the beginning of his rule and as a result he was able to prevail over the families who caused trouble in the princedom. An example was Banu Nakad, an influential family who persisted in intriguing against the Emir.

Al Shihabi recounts that the Emir in the pretext of bestowing favors on Banu Nakad invited them to his palace. Two other influential families at the time, Banu Imad and Banu Jumblat, allies of Emir Bashir, conspired to kill them.

As Banu Nakad entered the palace, they were killed and then the conspirators went to the village of the deceased in Abeyh where their belongings were completely confiscated. Their children who fled in the wilderness were caught, imprisoned, and tortured. Al Shihabi comments: "*It could be that God commanded to take revenge against Banu Nakad for their many atrocities.*"[48] Al Shihabi adds that they were stingy, criminals, and that they amassed money out of usury.

We see al Shihabi commenting on this incident showing his allegiance to Emir Bashir with utmost partiality in relating the events. There is no sense of distinguishing between what is right or wrong, a trend of a history where murder and revenge are the norms.

In his time, however, there took place two changes which were to weaken the basis of the princedom and affect its relations with the people. First the intervention of outside forces: 'Ali Bey of Egypt's army under his son Ibrahim Pasha in 1770 and then Bonaparte's expedition in 1799.

In 1830, Muhammad Ali's army conquered Syria. Haidar al Shihabi goes into detail in relating the historical events without any mention of the political and social repercussions of the policy of Bashir II when he became the pillar of Egyptian rule and aroused the discontent of his people, Druzes and Christians alike.

Haidar al Shihabi gives an ample picture of the history of Lebanon under the Shihabs, their struggle for power, their endeavors to please the different Ottoman governors, the influential families and the different factions in the princedom, Druzes, Shi'ites, Sunnis, and Christians and their role in shaping the history of the area. He also relates about the coming of the French to Acre and Emir Bashir's decision not to side either with Bonaparte or with al Jazzar, governor of Acre. He also relates about the friendship between the British general Smith and Bashir. The former interceded for Emir Bashir in front of the Ottoman Sultan, who expressed his readiness to help the latter against al Jazzar who at that time was causing the utmost trouble to Bashir II. This trouble with al Jazzar took a different shape in 1800 when the different factions in Lebanon were united against al Jazzar.

At that time, Jurjus Baz, who was allied to al Jazzar, decided to side with Emir Bashir and they together were able to defeat al Jazzar's soldiers.[49]

Al Shihabi does not comment here, but it is insinuated that unity of the Lebanese is the only way to obliterate the greed of the colonizers. What is significant in al Shihabi's account is his concern with European history, not only with Napoleon's expedition to Egypt where he relied on Niqula al Turk's history,[50] but also with an account of the French Revolution, the deposition and execution of Louis the XVI, and the rise of Bonaparte.

Al Shihabi goes into detail describing the execution of the king and mentions his courage in facing death. He describes the discontent of the people, but neglects the intellectual factors that led to the revolution. When he reaches Bonaparte, he shows his admiration for his personality and vigor and enumerates his victories describing him as a ferocious lion, unique person, and a valiant hero.[51]

Al Shihabi continues to enumerate the achievements of Bonaparte in invading Malta, his conflict with the British who stepped in to warn the Egyptians against the French and delves into the reasons of the British–French conflict and the aspiration of the French to reach India.[52] What draws attention here is al Shihabi's new endeavor to go into causes and effects, revealing an interest in the European and an awareness of the entanglement of the policy of the area with international affairs.

As mentioned earlier, al Shihabi's account is taken from Niqula al Turk's description of the French expedition to Egypt with some modifications. Al Shihabi selects and at certain times summarizes what is detailed in Al Turk's writing. He stresses the Egyptians' lack of confidence in the French though the latter manifested their allegiance to the teachings of Islam. He says: "The French resorted to various tricks and methods as their profession of Islam, their denial of Christianity, their allegiance to liberty and that in agreement with the Ottoman Empire they entered the land of Egypt ..."[53]

Al Shihabi goes on to show his admiration for the French. He says:

"... The French were Western people, remarkably patient and distinguished from other people in their conduct ... they propagated justice and good governance which encompassed completely the true law. In spite of this, the hearts of the Islamic people were not secure and rancor in their hearts remained prominent. They wished them disaster and destruction. This prompted the prince of the armies to fear so he resorted to tricky gentleness and compassion to attract the hearts and reach his goal. This renowned prince was

a lion among the lions, special of his kind, great among great men, wise and aware of the atrocities of times."[54]

As was mentioned before, al Shihabi admires the French and values Bonaparte's personality and vigor. He also seems to side with the French against the Egyptians and the Ottoman Empire. This tendency was prevalent among the Christian historians of that era.

This admiration for Napoleon and the French was truly manifested while al Shihabi was describing the defeat of the French at Acre in 1798. Al Shihabi goes into detail, describing the valor of the French armies and the intervention of General Sidney Smith to convince them to retreat. General Smith warned them that the aim of the directory in Paris was their destruction and that all kingdoms rallied against them. Smith promised them safe arrival to their country if they retreated. Hearing these words, the French were convinced, and the resistance halted.

Al Shihabi praises Bonaparte's wisdom and the devotion of the French soldiers toward him, his wisdom in accepting the circumstances and managing his retreat,[55] and the devotion of the French soldiers despite the catastrophes that they went through. He writes: *"Despite the fears and the calamities that they encountered, they remained strangely obedient, admiring and loving the prince of armies for he was like a god to obey his command, enduring his bitterness and constantly praising and thanking him."*[56]

After four months away from Egypt, Bonaparte arrived back in Cairo. Al Shihabi describes this entry a triumph. This triumph, however, was short lived, for Bonaparte had to face new opposition by the Ottomans. At the Battle of Abukir, however, Bonaparte was triumphant in capturing the pasha of Rumelia who joined Murad Bey and his son and other officers. To appease the Egyptians who desired victory for the Muslims, Bonaparte constantly demonstrated his allegiance and support of the Islamic religion.

Describing Bonaparte's departure from Egypt, al Shihabi concentrates on the prince of the armies' tactics and ruses, tactics in his generosity to General Smith and then in asking that he be allowed to send three small ships to France. Smith agreed and Bonaparte succeeded and with the dismay of General Smith, Bonaparte was able to escape to France. Al Shihabi comments:

"Bonaparte escaped thanks to his experience, his excessive awareness, and his exalted wisdom. He seized the opportunity to escape as the bird is released from his cage. Thanks to God's bounty, he escaped from the English enemies and reached Paris. He saved

himself in managing this matter and his influence is a miracle and one of the wonders of time. People then wondered considering what happened as a strange matter and an indication of his fortunate destiny."⁵⁷

Al Shihabi again expresses his admiration for Bonaparte and is with the French against the British. He relates the events in detail, mentioning Bonaparte's correspondence with General Kleber and promising him to return after fourteen months or else the French would reach an agreement directed by the British to give the land back to the Egyptians.

What draws attention in this context is al Shihabi's detailed account of the events and the ample information he provides in giving a full picture of the period he was living in. When delving into causes and effects, he cannot hide his partiality toward the Shihabis or the French. He leaves the reader at the end with unexplained questions concerning Bonaparte's decision to leave Egypt. Was it a result of the situation of his army, his defeat at Acre, the British, or the hostility and the attitude of the Egyptians toward the French and Christianity?

Acknowledgments

Parts of this chapter were originally published as "A Vision of a Historian: Hanania al Munayyir in *al Durr al Marsuf fi Hawadith al Shuf*," *Collectanea Christiana Orientalia* 13 (2017): 1–131.

Notes

1 Hanania al Munayyir was a Roman Catholic priest, a historian, a physician, and a poet. His works includes a *History of the Basilic Order*, *Bkirki Manuscript* on the history of Lebanon from 1736 till 1801, a *Commentary on the Beliefs of the Druzes*, translated into French by Henry Guys, *A Summary of the Proverbs of King Solomon*, *A Collection of Proverbs from Lebanon and Damascus*, *A Collection of Maqamat* and a book of poetry. See Introduction in *al-Durr al-Marsuf fi Hawadith al-Shuf*, ed. by Ignatius Sarkis (Gros Bros, 1984), 3, 17; See also Georg Graf, *Geschichte Der Christlichen Arabischen Literatur* (Vatican City: Biblioteca Apostolica Vaticana, 1949), 242–244. I am also using an undated edition for *al-Durr al-Marsuf* by the same editor. It contains additional information worth mentioning. I will refer to it as *Masadir*.
2 See the discussion in Kamal Salibi, *Maronite Historians of Mediaeval Lebanon* (Beirut: AUB Faculty of Arts and Sciences, Oriental Series 34, 1959); Usama Makdisi, *The Culture of Sectarianism* (Berkeley, CA: University of California Press, 2000), 40–41.

38 *Neo-Chroniclers*

3 On the monastery of Shwayr as an intellectual center and a precursor of Arab Nahda, see Carsten-Michael Walbiner, "Monastic Reading and Learning in Eighteenth Century Bilad al Sham: Some Evidence from the Monastery of Al Shuwayr (Mount Lebanon)," *Arabica*, TS 1, Fasc 4 (Brill, 2004), 462–477.

4 Al Munayyir lists the important families according to their rank and gives a detailed picture of the influential families at that time. See al Munayyir, *al-Durr*, 127–131.

5 See Kamal Salibi, "A History of Conflict and Consensus," edited by Nadim Shehadeh and Dana Haffar Mills (London: The Centre for Lebanese Studies, 1992), 5–6; This will eventually lead to a culture of sectarianism *which was already existent before the nineteenth century*. See the discussion in Usama Makdisi, *The Culture of Sectarianism*, 1–14. On the battle of 'Ayn Dara, see Ahmad Haydar al Shihabi, *al Ghurar al Hisan fi Akhbar abna' al Zaman*, ed. by Asad Rustum and Fuad Afram al Bustani (Beirut: Lebanese University Publications, 1969), 9–14.

6 Kamal Salibi, *The Modern History of Lebanon* (1999), 8–9.

7 Al Munayyir, *al Durr*, 18–21.

8 See Hayden V. White, *The Content of the Form: Narrative Discourse and Historical Representation* (Baltimore, MD: John Hopkins University Press, 1987), 1–25.

9 On the consequence of this rift, see Tannus al Shidiaq, *Akhbar al A'yan fi Jabal Lubnan* (Beirut: Nazir Abbud, 1997), 185–187; Mikhail Mishaqa, *Murder, Mayhem, Pillage and Plunder*, trans. by Wheeler Thackston (New York, NY: State University Press, 1988), 289–298, n. 51–52.

10 Al Munayyir, *al Durr*, 114.

11 Al Munayyir, *al Durr*, 118–119.

12 See the discussion in Kamal Salibi, *The Modern History of Lebanon*, 18–52. Also, Yasin Sweid, *Al Imarah al Shihabiah fi Jabal Lubnan*, edited by Adel Ismail *in Lubnan fi Tarikhihi wa Turathihi* ("Lebanon: its History and Culture") (Beirut: s.n., 1993), 307–333.

13 Al Munayyir, *Al Durr*, 65.

14 See Bernard Heyberger, *Hindiyya, Mistique et Criminelle* (Paris: Aubier, 2001). Also, Bernard Hykberger, *Les Chretiens du Proche Orient au temps de la reforme Catholique* (Paris: Ecole Francaise de Rome, 1994), 473–474.

15 Al Munayyir, *Al Durr*, 67.

16 Al Munayyir, *Al Durr*, 60.

17 Al Munayyir, *Al Durr*, 60.

18 Al Munayyir, *Al Durr*, 57–58.

19 Al Munayyir, *Masadir*, 34.

20 AL Munayyir, *Masadir*, 77.

21 Al Munayyir, *Masadir*, 152.

22 The king's son visited Beirut. The Muslims were afraid of a conspiracy and feared that the Europeans might besiege the city again. One of those present, an old blind shaykh, volunteered to get rid of the boy. He appeared like a beggar asking for charity and when the lad was preoccupied to respond, the shaykh attacked him together with the other Muslims that were with him. The king of Venice attacked Beirut and punished its inhabitants. Al Munayyir, *Masadir*, 51.

23 Al Munayyir, *al Dur*, 50–52.

Neo-Chroniclers 39

24 The seat of governorship at the time of Banu Tannukh and before them was in B'akline. The village lacked water, but on the other side of the valley there was a forest where a fountain of water was found. At the top of that forest was a Christian convent which was ruined throughout the years. The Christians were weak and were not able to restore it. See Al Munayyir, *Masadir*, 53.
25 Al Munayyir, *Masadir*, 52.
26 Tannus al-Shidyak, *Akhbar al Ayan fi Jabal Lubnan*, ed. by Maroun Raad (Beirut: Dar Nazir Abbud, 1997), 29.
27 Al Munayyir, *Masadir*, 23.
28 Al Munayyir, *Masadir*, 105.
29 Ahmad Beydoun, *Identité Confessionnelle et Temps Sociales Chez les Historiens Libanais Contemporains* (Beirut: Université Libanaise, 1989), 68. The translation is mine.
30 Nader el-Bizri, "Modernity, Tradition, and Renewal in Arab Thought: A Review Essay of Saud M.S. Al-Tamamy's *Averroes, Kant and the Origin of the Enlightenment" Journal of the Society for Contemporary Thought and the Islamic World, SCTIV Review* (Jan. 2015).
31 Al Munayyir, *Masadir*, 127.
32 Al Munayyir, *Masadir*, 127.
33 For al Turk's life, see Georg Graf, *Geschichte der christlichen arabischen Literatur*, Vol. 3 (Vatican City: Biblioteca Apostolica Vatican, 1949), 251–252; Nakoula El Turk, *Histoire de l'Expedition des Franrcais en Egypte*, trans. M. Desgrange (Paris: Aine, 1839); Jack Crabbs, *The Writing of History in Nineteenth Century Egypt* (Cairo: American University Press, 1984), 59.
34 Al Turk, *Mudhakkarat*, 5–6.
35 Al Turk, *Mudhakkarat*, 32.
36 Al Turk, *Mudhakkarat*, 2.
37 Al Turk, *Mudhakkarat*, 145–146.
38 Al Turk, *Mudhakkarat*, 31.
39 Al Turk, *Mudhakkarat*, 24.
40 See Albert Hourani, "Historians of Lebanon" *in Historians of the Middle East*, ed. by Bernard Lewis and P.M. Holt (London: Oxford University Press, 1962), 226–245.
41 The publication used in this study is titled *Lubnan fi ahd al Umara al Shihabiyyin* ("Lebanon at the time of the Shihani Princes") (Beirut: Lebanese University publication, 1969).
42 Banu Shihab was descendants of Banu Man in the female line. See Haidar Al Shihabi, *Lubnan fi ahd al umara al Shihabiin*, 4.
43 Haidar al Shihabi, *Lubnan fi ahd al umara al Shihabiin*, 7–8.
44 Haidar al Shihabi, *Lubnan fi Ahd al Umara al Shihabiin*, 8.
45 On the Battle of Ayndara and its importance, see Kamal Salibi, *The Modern History of Lebanon*, 8.
46 Al Shihabi relied on his private memoirs, the documents he had access to official documents, correspondence between the Ottoman government and the Wali's of the mountain, and, as mentioned before, from contemporary historians such as Hanania al Munayyir, Rufail Karameh al Himsi, Niqula al Turk, and others. See the introduction in Emir Haidar Ahmad al Shihabi, *Lubnan fi Ahd al umara al Shihabiyyin*, Vol. 1.

40 Neo-Chroniclers

47 Haidar al Shihabi, *Lubnan fi Ahd al Umara al Shihabiin*, 147.
48 Haidar al Shihabi, *Lubnan fi Ahd al Umara al Shihabiin*, 183–184.
49 Haidar al Shihabi, *Lubnan fi Ahd al Umara al Shihabiin*, 211.
50 Albert Hourani in *Historians of the Middle East*, 232.
51 Haidar al Shihabi, *Lubnan fi Ahd al Umara al Shihabiin*, 219.
52 Haidar al Shihabi, *Lubnan fi Ahd al Umara al Shihabiin*, 220–221.
53 Haidar al Shihabi, *Lubnan fi ahd al Umara al Shihabiin*, 235.
54 Haidar al Shihabi, *Lubnan fi Ahd al Umara al Shihabiin*, 235.
55 See: Haidar al Shihabi, *Lubnan fi Ahd al Umara al Shihabiin*, 268.
56 Haidar al Shihabi, *Lubnan fi Ahd al Umara al Shihabiin*, 267–268.
57 Al Shihabi, *Lubnan fi Ahd al Umara al Shihabiin*, 281.

Reference List

Al Munayyir, Hanania. *Al-Durr al-Marsuf fi Hawadith al-Shuf*, ed. by Ignatius Sarkis. Beirut: Dar al Raid al Arabi, 1984.

Al-Shidyak, Tannus. *Akhbar al Ayan fi Jabal Lubnan*, ed. by Maroun Raad. Beirut: Dar Nazir Abbud, 1997.

Al Shihabi, Ahmad Haydar. *al Ghurar al Hisan fi Akhbar abna' al Zaman*, ed. by Asad Rustum and Fuad Afram al Bustani. Beirut: Lebanese University Publications, 1969.

Al Shihabi, Haidar Ahmad. *Lubnan fi ahd al Umara al Shihabiyyin*. Beirut: Lebanese University Publications, 1969.

Beydoun, Ahmad. *Identité Confessionnelle et Temps Sociales Chez les Historiens Libanais Contemporains*. Beirut: Université Libanaise, 1989.

Crabbs, Jack. *The Writing of History in Nineteenth Century Egypt*. Cairo: American University Press, 1984.

El-Bizri, Nader. "Modernity, Tradition, and Renewal in Arab Thought: A Review Essay of Saud M.S. Al-Tamamy's *Averroes, Kant and the Origin of the Enlightenment*." *Journal of the Society for Contemporary Thought and the Islamic World, SCTIV Review* (Jan. 2015).

El Turk, Nakoula. *Histoire de l'Expedition des Franrcais en Egypte*, trans. M. Desgrange. Paris: Aine, 1839.

Graf, Georg. *Geschichte Der Christlichen Arabischen Literatur*, Vol. 3. Vatican City: Biblioteca Apostolica Vaticana, 1949.

Heyberger, Bernard. *Hindiyya, Mistique et Criminelle*. Paris: Aubier, 2001.

———. *Les Chretiens du Proche Orient au temps de la reforme Catholique*. Paris: Ecole Francaise de Rome, 1994.

Hourani, Albert. "Historians of Lebanon." In *Historians of the Middle East*, ed. by Bernard Lewis and P.M. Holt, 226–245. London: Oxford University Press, 1962.

Makdisi, Usama. *The Culture of Sectarianism*. Berkeley, CA: University of California Press, 2000.

Mishaqa, Mikhail. *Murder, Mayhem, Pillage and Plunder*, trans. by Wheeler Thackston. New York, NY: State University Press, 1988.

Salibi, Kamal. "A History of Conflict and Consensus," edited by Nadim Shehadeh and Dana Haffar Mills. London: The Centre for Lebanese Studies, 1992.

———. *Maronite Historians of Mediaeval Lebanon*. Beirut: AUB Faculty of Arts and Sciences, Oriental Series 34, 1959.

———. *The Modern History of Lebanon*. New York, NY: Caravan Books, 1999.

Sweid, Yasin. *Al Imarah al Shihabiah fi Jabal Lubnan*, edited by Adel Ismail in *Lubnan fi Tarikhihi wa Turathihi* ("Lebanon: its History and Culture"), 307–333. Beirut: s.n., 1993.

Walbiner, Carsten-Michael. "Monastic Reading and Learning in Eighteenth Century Bilad al Sham: Some Evidence from the Monastery of Al Shuwayr (Mount Lebanon)." *Arabica*, TS 1, Fasc 4. Brill, 2004: 462–477.

White, Hayden V. *The Content of the Form: Narrative Discourse and Historical Representation*. Baltimore, MD: John Hopkins University Press, 1987.

3 Biographical Writing

In her book, *The Art of Biography*, Virginia Woolf states, "*by telling us the true facts, by sifting the little from the big, and shaping the whole so that we perceive the outline, the biographer does more to stimulate the imagination than any poet or novelist save the greatest.*"[1]

Biographical writing enables us to understand the nature and functioning of human groups by knowing about the individuals who composed it. Biography is history, for studying individuals, their actions and motivations, we penetrate into an understanding of the society in its various aspects. It is here that biographers, as historians, are able to discover motivation, and to place their subjects fully in the context of their political, social, and economic times and, as Robert Rotberg puts it, "*Without biography of all kinds, especially those that are sensitive and responsible, the historical enterprise would be far less informed, and far less complete.*"[2]

Biographical writing, then, is a tool, not only to discover individual life stories, but to place the individual into the social, political, and intellectual context and come to an understanding of the society they were living in. This can be achieved through both kinds of biographical writing, autobiography and biography.

3.1 Autobiography: Abdallah Qarali (1674–1742)

Autobiography is a source of cultural, social, as well as individual history. In order to explain a meaning, to explain a life, the biographer recreates the social and cultural as well as individual context that surrounds his life, perceiving and continuing the dialogue between himself and the world. In presenting their individual histories they employ a culturally acceptable representation of self or self-conception. Autobiography includes public as private experiences, a combination of "memoir," an individualistic public

DOI: 10.4324/9781003023432-4

record and confessions – a private record of private experiences as in the case of Abdallah Qarali who presented an image of the self-synthesizing public and private histories in accordance with the ideals of eighteenth-century Lebanon that focused on the exemplary self. This self fits a preconceived pattern of a religious person who concentrates on Divine providence thus representing an ideal type, and at the same time enabling the readers through his experiences to understand a century where, in spite of its intrigues, emphasized universality of principles rather than individual importance.

An example of autobiography then is the memoirs of Abdallah Qarali. These memoirs do not only express a spiritual experience, but reveal a whole life of strife and toil where work, achievements, worship, and suffering go hand in hand, leading to the founding of the Maronite religious order, a turning point in the history of the Maronites and Lebanon. History and spirituality are combined in these memoirs to produce an autobiography – a life story within a historical, societal, religious, and intellectual context.

Abdallah Qarali is the founder of the Maronite monastic orders in Lebanon.[3] Qarali delves into his inner self to express his feelings while relating the history of the founding of these orders and introducing other members of the community together with the religious life at this initial period of Maronite history.

It is in this context that Qarali will be dealt with: as an autobiographer, a biographer, and a historian. Qarali relates the history of the Maronite orders providing information about his experience with the other members of the community, his superiors, and his relation with Rome and the Church authorities. Qarali reveals the details of the communal life in these monasteries with its political, social, and intellectual preoccupations and conflicts. He, at the same time, succeeds in describing the struggle between his attachment to the glories of the world and his love of God.

Qarali starts his memoirs uttering the following words:

"I the inconsiderable among the superiors, Abd Allah the bishop of Beirut, of Aleppian descent and the Lebanese monk yearned to the monastic life as soon as I reached the age of adulthood. My father Mikhail prevented me for my ignorance about the ways of people and the absence from my native land. I remained perplexed in my thinking, occupying myself at times with the world forgetting priesthood, and at other time spending my time in studying books and reading till I reached twenty-one years of my age."[4]

Qarali starts by mentioning himself. The word "I" expresses a sense of self-awareness surrounded by a pure spiritual frame, describing himself as insignificant, showing his humility while being cognizant about the weaknesses of human beings and their evil tendencies, and expressing at the same time the frailty of man and his inability to find his identity except in his creator.

Qarali's self-awareness is grounded in traditional religious foundations and inherited conventions, the most important being to obey one's parents. This is how he mentions his father and his compliance with his wishes when the idea of priesthood occurred to him.[5] Qarali says that his father complied with his wishes on condition that he first visits Jerusalem then pass by Lebanon to examine his willingness to live there. In this way he will appear as a visitor to these places and not as one who has renounced the ministry.[6]

Qarali, as a historian, goes into detail in narrating and describing the founding of the monasteries, the new rules he introduced, and the schools he established beside those monasteries.[7] As an autobiographer and a biographer, he does not hesitate to tell the truth about himself and the others. In this sense, one can see the elements of history, autobiography, and biography intermingling in his memoirs. He criticizes others while criticizing himself at the same time. This occurred when he was accusing the superior Jibrail Hawwa[8] for his interference in all matters, the thing that caused disagreement between him and the other procurators. He recalled,

> *"In general, we were all inexperienced and subject to making mistakes because of our ignorance of virtue and our lack of self-mortification. There was no one to lead us to perfection. The worm of hatred continued slightly to graze our orchard, the congregation's grumbling and muttering increased from time to time till the superior hated the procurators' position and most of the monks hated his obedience. But the fear of God and the people preserved us from complete downfall. We would entertain and console each other and encourage each other, too. At times we would forget all matters and desire obedience and the will of God, and at other times we would fall back to boredom and anxiety."*[9]

Qarali is writing about the past seizing the opportunity to describe the struggle in his divided soul between virtue and depravity, between succumbing to one's desires and walking on the road of perfection. Qarali's description of this struggle revealed his power and skill to penetrate into the inner depths of the soul to uncover its secrets:

"*the love of leadership started to tempt me knowing that I can replace the superior once he is deposed.*"[10] He adds, "*It is understood by every knowledgeable person that because of our lack of virtue and perfection we used to offend the superior's obedience.*"[11]

Qarali goes on to relate how he was obliged to accept his ordination as a bishop from the Patriarch Awwad because he feared him. He says: "*Cowardice took possession of me, I sacrificed my heart, nothing at all distracted me, I did not know how to appease myself in hoping and relying on God, and that He the Almighty is the origin of death and life. He lowers people's positions and he raises others from the dunghill.*"[12]

Qarali examines and unveils himself, exposing his cowardice and fear from a fellow human being. This fear is a result of his love of power and his frail belief in God. In other words, the author is here trying while exposing his weakness to convey an idea about the inability of man to unite between love of the world and the love of God and that a person loses himself in the world and finds himself only in God the source of his existence. Qarali's memoirs are a confessional autobiography where the writer, while observing, becomes himself the object of investigation, remembrance, and contemplation. He is stating a record of a transformation of errors by values – the values of the age he lives in.[13]

Qarali's awareness of himself appeared not only in this direct psychological nudity, but also in his narration of the different events where we see him as an autobiographer revealing his tendencies and as a biographer in describing the other members in the community. In 1715, he wrote concerning Patriarch Awwad: "*In 1715, Patriarch Awwad started playing with our order, negligent with the dissatisfied monks to encourage them to leave the congregation, then taking a malignant appearance to prove that he is against this trouble.*" Qarali continues: "*He would flatter me without knowing his intention.*" Among his flatteries he told me: "*I want you to ask a favor from me to confirm our friendship.*"[14] He repeated this several times. I then asked him to give an acquittal paper to release the monks from the money that his parents gave to the governor of the country, assuring him that my intention was only to keep our accounts clear for the future and what might happen after our death."[15]

This does not only reveal Qarali's wisdom in settling matters and his understanding of the patriarch's intention and his ability to deal with him on practical and pragmatic grounds. It also describes Patriarch Awwad's tendencies and personality. At the same time, Qarali's awareness of himself, his spirituality, and his life of mortification did not prevent him from understanding the realities as they were and situate them in their time, place, and context. Self-awareness in this sense appeared to move in two parallel directions: a spiritual dimension and a worldly dimension. Qarali continues: "*We did not share a spiritual love with the mentioned patriarch, but a love of worldly behavior only.*"[16] The author here does not contradict himself, but seems to find himself in the teaching of the New Testament: "Be as shrewd as snakes and harmless as doves."[17]

Self-awareness for Qarali is also in a specific sense of identity. This was apparent at the beginning of his memoirs when he mentioned that he is the bishop of Beirut, of Alleppian descent, and a Lebanese monk."[18] In this he considers the place he lives as a vital element in determining his identity. Aleppo is his birthplace, where he was born and raised, and Lebanon is where he fulfilled his monastic vocation. This was grounded in Qarali's being, for he recorded in 1705:

"*This year I found it advisable to call our congregation the Lebanese Order, and to refer to the monks as Lebanese for they are alleged to Mount Lebanon as we call the monks of Mount Carmel Carmelites. The reason is that I knew by insinuation that certain brethren did not find it commendable to refer to Aleppo in naming the congregation since it is associated with Alleppian people. When I entered in 1707, I asked the patriarch to call us by this name. He accepted and corresponded with us.*"[19]

The author continues: "*We relinquished the idea of Rome from our heads and became convinced of our own country.*"[20] "Our country" signifies Lebanon, in particular. The sense of Lebanese identity is clearly manifested here.

Qarali is informing us about the history of the founding of the monastic order while penetrating into the innermost secrets of the convents and introducing the reader to the different personalities there. Qarali is the actor and the observer in that he puts a deliberate distance between himself and his subject, a pose of objectivity and authority at the same time. This is how he gave a description of one of the founders, Jibrail Hawwa, when he writes: "*He used at times to deal with reprehensible issues harming his leadership for it was his nature to meddle in all things and advise every person in what he is doing, even with the cook, the shoe maker, and the gardener.*"[21] Jibrail, according to Qarali, used to absent himself for days without Qarali's permission. Qarali continues:

"*I was angry and I scolded him. Anger surmounted me because he answered me in a nasty way. This made things worse with me and with some of the brethren who started hurting him with words while I showed looseness in dealing with the matter fearing that I might antagonize them. That was cowardice on my part and a human weakness lest Gibrail get his way to separate me from my brethren and destroy the basic rule. As a result, Gibrail left the congregation and accused us in front of the bishop, who sent people to investigate about the matter."*

Qarali confesses, *"I became submissive out of my anxiety and wrote to the patriarch acknowledging my mistakes against Hawwa and expressing my willingness that Hawwa come back to the convent as its superior."* Hawwa refused, fearing that the brethren in the convent would not accept this solution. The result was that Qarali was to direct Mar Elisha and Hawwa Mar Moura. The monks were to choose where to go. In the end, one hundred and eleven followed Qarali and only one followed Hawwa.[22]

This division did not last long for before the end of the year Hawwa had a dispute with his bishop, Jirjis Binyamin of Ihdin. Qarali does not hesitate to mention that the bishop hit Hawwa and they both appealed to the patriarch who did not support Hawwa in any aspect. In fact, the bishop prevented Hawwa from having any liberty in his convent to an extent that he did not allow him to designate the word Jesuit on his congregation. Hawwa, abandoned by most of his monks, travelled to Malta and later to Rome.[23]

Qarali plays the role of the authentic historian, biographer, and autobiographer. As a historian, he states the facts as they occurred, allowing the readers to penetrate into the secrets of the monastic life. He describes reality as it is revealing the truth without trying to show only what is positive in the monastic life. Life in convents is similar to every other life in the society. There are times of peace and moments of conflict. Human nature is the same in the convent and outside the convents. As a biographer, he gives an ample picture of the different personalities, describing their actions and giving examples to make people profit from the lessons of the past.

Qarali, for example, admires Jibrail Farhat, who was respected by the priests as a convent superior and a scholar in Arabic language, poetry, and eloquence. Qarali relates how Jibrail separated from him in 1700 and went to teach the children in Zgharta, then came back in 1705 because of his sickness. The doctors prevented him from living in Zgharta because of the bad weather and the climate. Qarali continues: *"We appointed him as superior for his wisdom and concern; he was hot tempered, serious in his endeavors, firmly educated, a philosopher and a poet greatly respected amongst the elderly and the youngest for his eloquence and understanding."*[24]

Qarali, the biographer, then draws a vivid picture of the different personalities assessing their character and describing their actions and reactions in the different situations. As an autobiographer, he is uniting the external circumstances and internal thoughts and feelings relating his story about the events in a chronological sequence and basing his narration on verified facts.[25] This is how one detects Qarali the historian with his great measure of self-consciousness while narrating the history of the founding of the Lebanese Maronite orders. He relates all the difficulties encountered whether inside or outside the congregation and does not hesitate to mention, for example, his experience in the convent of Tamish where he spent 3 months. He wanted with Yusuf al Batn to live in that convent on condition that the nuns be asked to live in a separate convent. All agreed, but the bishop refused saying that the convent would be destroyed without the nuns.[26]

Qarali wrote in a language similar to the classical. He related the history of the congregation and introduced different personalities in various circumstances, commenting and reflecting on the meaning and significance of events. He used analogy while describing the characters like when he referred to the Bible to clarify the meaning of a certain event that happened to him with the priest Yakoub. He wrote: *"His behavior was similar to St Peter's because at the times of our separation from Priest Hawwa, he used to say: I will not leave Priest Abdallah the superior till death ... He was the first to leave me."*[27]

Qarali refers to the Bible to compare and contrast and to explain his intentions. He writes his memoirs to relate the history of the Lebanese order to inform those coming after him about the culture and achievements of the past and at the same time to learn from these events and profit from their experiences. There is a sign of the historian's ego underpinning the narrative. The use of "I" and "myself" to interrupt the narrative and introduce the historian's personal comments or opinions on people and events becomes frequent enough to be noticeable. From this follows the temptation of being wiser after the event.[28] Qarali as a historian learned from the lessons of the past.

Qarali's memoirs are a historical document where autobiography, biography, and history intermingle and intertwine.[29] Qarali grasps the course of his experience in such a way as to bring to consciousness the basis of human life, namely the historical relations in which it is interwoven. What emerged is a didactic form of memoirs to describe a life journey confused by frequent misdirection and sometimes crises, but reaching at last a sense of perspective and integration.[30]

Qarali's memoirs reflect a genre of historical writing in eighteenth-century Lebanon. A spiritual memoirs[31] where Qarali is not writing to draw the attention to his individuality, feelings, sentiments, or intellectual developments, but aspiring toward a religious goal he has himself chosen and followed. One can detect here the importance of the community and the individual's concern to adapt to the society. This, however, did not prevent Qarali from examining himself and exposing his weaknesses, but instead of losing himself in a divided and dispersed being, he directed it toward the creator.

Qarali wrote his memoirs after a long experience in the monastic life. He was able to penetrate the depth of his being where the mystery of life was revealed to him. These are a result of a continuous struggle not only with other members of his community, but also with the ecclesiastical authorities in Rome and elsewhere. They are also an expression of a spiritual experience, a soul in solitude, penetrating into the depths of its being to know itself more fully and be related to an ultimate reality beyond the self, to come to a new awareness of the Divine and with it the glory of finding oneself in God.

3.2 Biography: Abbud al Sabbagh (d. 1799)

We move with Abbud al Sabbagh to biographical writing. Al Sabbagh was a Christian historian in eighteenth-century Lebanon. He left a manuscript in the Bibliotheque Nationale (Codex 46 10) entitled *al Rawd al Zahir fi Tarikh Daher*[32] ("The Blooming Garden in the History of Daher") in which he narrated the career of Daher al Umar, who ruled over Acre and northern Palestine in the third quarter of the eighteenth century (1750–1755).

In describing Daher's rise to power, his alliances with 'Ali Bey of Egypt and with the Russians, his relations with the local factions in *Bilad al-Shâm*, and with the Ottoman Empire, al Sabbagh gives not only a living portrait of Daher al Omar, but also of his two main associates, Ahmad Agha al Dinkizli and Ibrahim al Sabbagh. At the same time, he gives first-hand information about an important period in eighteenth-century Lebanon and in Bilad al Sham.

'Abbud al Sabbagh's biography of Daher al Umar distinguishes itself from the Christian historiographical trend in eighteenth-century Lebanon. While the other historians were mainly concerned with apologetics, the Antiochian Patriarchate and other ecclesiastical matters as well as with the social conditions of the Christian communities, we find in 'Abbud al Sabbagh's biography a purely secular and political history solely dedicated to the achievements of a Muslim ruler and his struggle for political power. Thus, after throwing light on the events of that period, the author succeeds in using history to support his conviction regarding two of Daher al Umar's associates, Ibrahim al Sabbagh, whose integrity is praised, and al Dinkizli, Daher's "bete noire," whose treachery is denounced as the main cause for the downfall of Daher al-Omar in 1775.

As a biographer, al Sabbagh has his special approaches to persons and events. He follows what one might call the *realistic* tendency which prompts him to take hold of all data of interest, and the *formative* tendency, which prompts him at other times to explain and interpret material. In this sense, he is both passive and active, a recorder and creator at the same time. He not only records the event as a historical phenomenon, but he makes it vibrate with meaning, thus giving a framework for biography which leads to a better understanding of the actor and the personalities who direct the events.

The author is mainly concerned with the career of an influential Muslim ruler, Daher al Umar, his rise to power and his downfall. He directs his narrative toward Daher's actions, his conflict with the Ottoman authorities, and the guilt of al Dinkizli in this drama.

Al Sabbagh describes Daher's rise to power, putting stress mainly on his ability in subduing the Bedouins, his challenge to the governor of Damascus, and his skill in dealing with the Ottoman central administration in Constantinople.

The author in his narrative gives a clear picture of Daher's openness to the outside world, his relations with Ali Bey of Egypt and the Russians and his involvement in international trade, mainly with the French merchants. Al Sabbagh mentions that Daher was popular among the French and every time he went to Acre, he got what he wanted from the French hostelry-Khan. Here we see how private details appear in al Sabbagh's narrative. He relates how Ali Bey wanted to go to Egypt in 1773 and enumerates the arguments that Daher used to persuade him not to return and warning him against Muhammad Abu'l Dahab[33] and his bad intentions.

Al Sabbagh weaves history into biography. While giving a portrait of Daher al Umar, he draws attention to the qualities that make a ruler consolidate or lose his state, to the good intentions of Ibrahim al Sabbagh and his loyalty to Daher al Umar, and lastly to the evil nature of al Dinkizli, thus blaming him for the disaster.

The author's primary concern is not to write a panegyric of the ruler, nor to talk without constraint about an admired figure or hero, but primarily to give information about an important period in the eighteenth century through an influential personality and his achievements, drawing a portrait of Daher while assessing the qualities which help a ruler maintain or lose his rule.

Daher is described as a powerful ruler who knows when and how to seize opportunities, to conclude beneficial alliances and to adapt his policy to the various circumstances. He was ready, for example, to ally himself with his enemies whenever that was necessary to maintain his power. Here al Sabbagh relates how after the death of Ali Bey of Egypt in 1773, he agreed to treat with the Druzes of Lebanon under Emir Yusuf al Shihabi because he needed allies at that time.

Daher became embroiled later on in the struggle with Ahmad Pasha al Jazzar[34] over Beirut. When the Russian vessels arrived, they were entrusted by Daher to attack. Al Sabbagh reports how Daher addressed the Russians:

> "Ali Bey is dead, but I am alive. The love that bound you with Ali Bey, can bind you now with me. The Druze Emir is my ally and the Jazzar cutinized against him in Beirut. If you desire, you can accompany my soldiers to Beirut and expel al Jazzar and I will give you six hundred bags that I will get from the Druze Emir."[35]

Al Sabbagh relates how al Jazzar was defeated and took refuge with Daher al Umar. Daher admired al Jazzar's courage and entrusted him in 1773 to collect the *miri* (taxes) from the region of Jerusalem, but, alas, al Jazzar betrayed Daher and intrigued against him.[36]

In recounting these details, Abbud al Sabbagh exposes Daher's personality in its prowess and strength as well as in its weakness. The fact that Daher was naïve enough to trust al Jazzar's loyalty and failed to understand his treachery, greed, and ambitions, shows the flaw in Daher's character.

Daher was defeated by the Ottomans and here al Sabbagh adds a romantic touch to the story of Daher showing the true nature of the hero at the moment of his downfall. Daher refused to escape with his soldiers because he was waiting for his concubine Aisha to accompany him. Aisha preferred to stay with al Dinkizli. Al Sabbagh writes:

> "Daher remained alone, the bullets falling on him. Aisha did not follow. He then marched for a quarter of an hour and then fell unconscious. His horse followed the other horses. The horsemen recognized the horse to be that of Daher. Daher remained on the ground unconscious until the Maghariba (North Africans) arrived. They cut off his head and took it to al Dinkizli who gave it to Hasan Pasha."[37]

Thus, Abbud al Sabbagh succeeds as a skillful biographer in giving an ample portrait of Daher in his strength and in his weakness. He pictures him as a merciless ruler when his interests seemed to be at stake. At the same time, Daher's iron will which subdued the local factions, perplexed the Ottoman Empire and the governors of Sidon and Damascus, succumbed at the end, and the story of Aisha brings the reader to the reality that great men and women also pass through phases of frailty, emotion, passions, and despair.

Al Sabbagh gives at the same time a portrait of Daher's associates, Ibrahim al Sabbagh and Ahmad Agha al Dinkizli, thus succeeding in portraying the secondary characters through the political events of the period, and in the context of their relationships with Daher al Umar.

The author pictures al Dinkizli as a malicious and opportunist person who never liked Daher and who betrayed him at the end. Al Dinkizli is presented as a man without principles, disloyal, and mean.[38]

Al Sabbagh, on the other hand, presents his relative Ibrahim al Sabbagh as an able physician and a good advisor to Daher al Umar. Ibrahim taught Daher the art of ruling which helped in the prosperity of the country. He prevented Daher from being tyrannical and putting pressure on the peasants and also supplied him with enough money to be sent as taxes to the Sublime Porte. Ibrahim was also, according to al Sabbagh, generous, brave, honest, and a loyal man. All this won him the admiration of Daher al Umar.[39]

The picture we get here of Ibrahim al Sabbagh is undoubtedly different from what we read in Volney and other contemporary chroniclers. Should we infer from this that the author is incapable of being objective while writing about his relative, Ibrahim al Sabbagh, it is our privilege. The significant thing, however, is that the author introduces us to another point of view and makes us aware of an important issue, namely the liberality of Daher al Umar and his readiness to collaborate with a Christian and put all his trust in him.

Thus, Abbud al Sabbagh is able as a biographer to portray the secondary characters while narrating the events. In this portrayal, he turns to history to explain human contact. The author may be insinuating a fact that not only are the ruler's own staff a major factor in the rise or decline of a state, but also and of equal importance is the shrewdness of the ruler in discerning the good advice from the bad one. In other words, Daher al Umar should have listened to Ibrahim al Sabbagh who continually warned him against al Dinkizli.

Al Sabbagh as a biographer is writing about the career of Daher al Umar which is a series of achievements in an important period in Bilad al Sham. Al Sabbagh gives valuable information about the contacts of

Daher al Umar with the French and English merchants and his good relations with them. He draws attention to the Western infiltration in the area which was in fact a cumulative process made up of innumerable contacts between the European traders and the local inhabitants in the economic, technological, and cultural fields. Al Sabbagh is a biographer who provides valuable historical information while describing Daher's openness to outside influences thus throwing some light on the process of change which started in the eighteenth century and received its impetus as a result of Western influences. It is an apology in defense of Ibrahim al Sabbagh, the loyal secretary, physician, and finance minister of Daher al Umar. It is at the same time an accusation against al Dinkizli, the villain who schemed, cheated, and betrayed.

The Blooming Garden in the History of Daher distinguishes al Sabbagh as a skillful biographer and a historian at the same time. Taking the above into consideration one can say that Abbud al Sabbagh's biography of Daher al Umar is a life story in a chronicle where the author is trying to narrate, entertain, meditate, and warn.

Acknowledgments

Parts of this chapter were originally published as "Abbud al Sabbagh and His Biography of Daher al 'Umar," *Parole de L'Orient* 24 (1999): 339–356.

Notes

1 Virginia Woolf, "The Art of Biography," in Woolf, *The Death of the Moth and Other Essays* (New York, NY, 1942), 192.
2 Robert I. Rotberg, *Journal of Interdisciplinary History*, XL 3, 2010, 305.
3 On the Memoirs genre and its relation to autobiography see: Maher Jarrar, "Mudakarat al muthaqaffin al injilyyin al Arab-Dirasat Tasnifiyyah," in *al Sirat al datiah fi Bilad al Sham*, ed. by Maher el Sharif and Qays al Zurli (Damascus: Dar al Mada and Institut Francais du Proche Orient, 2009).
4 Abdallah Qarali, *Mudakarrat*, in Joseph Qazzi, *Bidayat al Rahbanah al Lubnaniah* (Kaslik: Markaz al Nashr wa al Tawzi', 1988), 25. The translation is mine. Hereafter, Bidayat. On the life of Qarali, see: Louis Cheikho, *Kitab al Makhtoutat al Arabiah li Katabat al Nasraniah* (Beirut: Jesuit Publication House, 1924), 160–161; Jirjis Manash, "Tarkat al Sayid Jirmanus Farhat" (Beirut: *al Mashriq* (8), 1904), 354–361; Touma al Labboudi, "Sirat al ab Abdallah Qarali," Bidayat, 75–106. Georg Graf, *Geschichte Der Christlichen Arabischen Literatur* (Roma: Biblioteca Apostolica Vaticana, 1949), 406–428. The editor mentions that Al Mudakarat reached us in an incomplete form and in 71 pages.
5 *Bidayat*, 163
6 *Bidayat*, 25–26.

54 Biographical Writing

7   Qarali, *Bidayat*, 27–31; also, Boulos Qarali, *al La'ali' fi Hayat al Mitran Abdallah Qaral* (Bayt Shabab: Matbaat al Ilm. 1932), 41–42. The first school was in Mar Moura in Ihdin. There, Qarali used to teach the students under a walnut tree. The monks did not have the means to build a school at that time.
8   Jibrail Hawwa was one of the founders of the monastic order. He travelled from Aleppo to Lebanon in 1649. The third founder is Yusuf al Batn, who died when a rock fell on him in the Monastery of Dayr Quzhayya, *Bidayat*, 26.
9   Qarali, *Bidayat*, 33.
10 Qarali, *Bidayat*, 37.
11 Qarali, *Bidayat*, 37.
12 Qarali, *Bidayat*, 66.
13 See: *Autobiography: Essays Theoretical and Critical*, ed. by James Iney (Princeton, NJ: Princeton University Press, 1980); cf. *Essays in 18th Century Biography*, ed. by Philip B. Daghlian (Bloomington, IN: Indiana University Press, 1968).
14 *Bidayat*, 57–63.
15 Bishop Awwad was in Kisrawan. He used to express friendship to Qarali by lodging with him money about which the latter did not know its source. Qarali knew later from Bishop Jirjis Amin of Ihden disgraceful news concerning Bishop Awwad. Qarali told the Bishop about the money. The patriarch's family gave the money to the governor of the country to win his friendship and to prevent the new patriarch from taking it. The money was then taken by force, which caused harm and insults to the monks. Qarali, *Bidayat*, 55–65.
16 Qarali, *Bidayat*, 63. On the subject of self-awareness, see Jeremy Popkin, *History, Historians, and Autobiography* (Chicago, IL: University of Chicago Press, 2005).
17 Matthew 10:16. *The Restored New Testament – A New Translation* (New York, NY: W.W. Norton and Company, 2009).
18 Qarali, *Bidayat*, 25.
19 Qarali, *Bidayat*, 51–52.
20 Qarali, *Bidayat*, 60. Jibrail Hawwa, one of the founders, went to Rome and tried with the pope to found a convent for the Lebanese monks there. Qarali hesitated to send his priests, then he complied with the wishes of Hawwa. As a result, two monks went to Rome, but after a year they disagreed with Hawwa. In 1711, Qarali sent Jibrail Farhat the superior of the Convent of Mar Elijah to Rome with two clergymen who founded a separate convent there when they realized the impossibility of cooperating with Hawwa. Later, when facing trouble from other people, they came back to Lebanon. See Qarali, *Bidayat*, 53–60. On the subject of Lebanese identity in the eighteenth century, see: Hayat Bualuan, *Muarikhu Bilad al Sham fi al qarn al Thamin Ashar*, 206–207.
21 Qarali, *Bidayat*, 33.
22 Qarali, *Bidayat*, 43–44.
23 Qarali, *Bidayat*, 46–48.
24 Qarali, *Bidayat*, 50–52. Jibrail Farhat died in 1734. He was the superior of the diocese of Aleppo in 1725 and became known as Germanus Farhat. See Nuahd Razzouk, *Girmanus Farhat Hayatuhu wa Atharuhu* (al Kaslik, 1998); Anuti Usama, *al Harakat al Adabiyyah fi Bilad*

al Sham Khilal al Qarn al Thamin Ashar (Beirut: Dar al Talia, 1971), 118–121. On the monastic orders, see: Maraqi al Kamal al Rahbani, *Manshurat al Rahbaniah al Makhlisiah fi Yubiliha al Miawi al Thalith*, 1985; also, Abdallah Qarali, *al Misbah al Rahbany*, ed. Jurjus Mouani al Halabi (Beirut: Matabi, Samya, 1957).

25 On the identification of history with biography, see: Tarif Khalidi, *Arabic Historical Thought in the Classical Period* (1994), 207–221.
26 Qarali, *Bidayat*, 27–28. The monastic orders before Qarali were not organized. The monks did not abide by the rules of obedience and purity. They had their own ways in practicing religion. See Butrus Fahd, *Tarikh al Rahbaniah al Lubnaniah bi fi'raiha al al Halabi wal Lubnani* (Jounieh: Mataba'at al Karim, 1965), 1 and 116.
27 Qarali, *Bidayat*. Yakoub is from Ghazir. He followed Qarali, then Hawwa. In 1706, Qarali opened the convent of St John in Rihmayya and appointed the curate Yakoub as its superior. One day, while he was on a tour in a village, the people convinced him to send a priest to teach the children and expressed their desire in taking the Convent of Mar Elias. Curate Yakoub threatened Qarali that he would leave him if he does not comply with his demand. Later, however, he came back to Qarali.
28 See Tarif Khalidi, *Arabic Historical Thought in the Classical Period*, 200–204.
29 On the terms "Memoirs" and "Autobiography," see Maher Jarrar "Mudakarat al Muthaqaffin al Injiliyyin al Arab-Dirasat Tasnifiyat" in *al Sirat al datiah fi Bilad al Sham*, 8–10.
30 See: Sidonie Smith & Julia Watson, *Reading Autobiography* (Minneapolis: University of Minnesota Press, 2001), 83–110; Jeremy Popkin, *History, Historians and Autobiography* (Chicago, IL: Chicago University Press, 2005), 11–32.
31 On spiritual autobiography, see: G.A. Starr, *Defoe and Spiritual Autobiography* (Princeton, NJ: Princeton University Press, 1965), 1–50.
32 The manuscript was edited by Abu Nahl Usama Muhammad in 2017 (Noor Publishing House). I am using the manuscript as the book is out of print.
33 A Mamluk who controlled Egypt in the eighteenth century under Ali Bey.
34 Governor of Acre in the eighteenth century.
35 Al Sabbagh, *Al Rawd*, 53–55.
36 Al Sabbagh, *Al Rawd*, 70.
37 Al Sabbagh, *Al Rawd*, 72.
38 Al Sabbagh, *Al Rawd*, 67.
39 Al Sabbagh, *Al Rawd*, 26–27.

Reference List

Al Labboudi, Touma. "Sirat al ab Abdallah Qarali," *Bidayat*, 75–106.

Al Rahbani, Maraqi al Kamal. *Manshurat al Rahbaniah al Makhlisiah fi Yubiliha al Miawi al Thalith*. 1985.

Anuti, Usama. *al Harakat al Adabiyyah fi Bilad al Sham Khilal al Qarn al Thamin Ashar*. Beirut: Dar al Talia, 1971.

56 Biographical Writing

Barnstone, Willis, trans. *The Restored New Testament – A New Translation*. New York, NY: W.W. Norton and Company, 2009.

Cheikho, Louis. *Kitab al Makhtoutat al Arabiah li Katabat al Nasraniah*. Beirut: Jesuit Publication House, 1924.

Daghlian, Philip B., ed. *Essays in 18th Century Biography*. Bloomington, IN: Indiana University Press, 1968.

Fahd, Butrus. *Tarikh al Rahbaniah al Lubnaniah bi fi'raiha al al Halabi wal Lubnani*. Jounieh: Mataba'at al Karim, 1965.

Graf, Georg. *Geschichte Der Christlichen Arabischen Literatur*. Rome: Biblioteca Apostolica Vaticana, 1949.

Iney, James, ed. *Autobiography: Essays Theoretical and Critical*. Princeton, NJ: Princeton University Press, 1980.

Jarrar, Maher. "Mudakarat al muthaqaffin al injilyyin al Arab-Dirasat Tasnifiyyah." In *al Sirat al datiah fi Bilad al Sham*, ed. by Maher el Sharif and Qays al Zurli. Damascus: Dar al Mada and Institut Francais du Proche Orient, 2009.

Khalidi, Tarif. *Arabic Historical Thought in the Classical Period*. Cambridge: Cambridge University Press, 1994.

Manash, Jirjis. "Tarkat al Sayid Jirmanus Farhat," 354–361. In *al Mashriq* (8), 1904.

Popkin, Jeremy. *History, Historians, and Autobiography*. Chicago, IL: University of Chicago Press, 2005.

Qarali, Abdallah. *al Misbah al Rahbany*, ed. Jurjus Mouani al Halabi. Beirut: Matabi, Samya, 1957.

Qarali, Abdallah. *Mudakarrat*. In Joseph Qazzi, *Bidayat al Rahbanah al Lubnaniah*. Kaslik: Markaz al Nashr wa al Tawzi', 1988.

Qarali, Boulos. *al La'ali' fi Hayat al Mitran Abdallah Qaral*. Bayt Shabab: Matbaat al Ilm, 1932.

Razzouk, Nuahd. *Girmanus Farhat Hayatuhu wa Atharuhu*. Al Kaslik, 1998.

Rotberg, Robert I. *Journal of Interdisciplinary History*, XL 3, 2010.

Smith, Sidonie and Julia Watson. *Reading Autobiography*. Minneapolis: University of Minnesota Press, 2001.

Starr, G.A. *Defoe and Spiritual Autobiography*. Princeton, NJ: Princeton University Press, 1965.

Woolf, Virginia. "The Art of Biography." In Virginia Woolf, *The Death of the Moth and Other Essays*. New York, NY, 1942.

4 Apologetic History
The Maronite Question

We move now to another form of historical writing, namely apologetics. We will not delve into doctrinal dialectics, but will focus instead on a few historical facts which caused since the time of Estephan al Duwaihi dialectical arguments which can be fairly described as "the Maronite Question."[1] The two historians who will be dealt with here are Yusuf Simaan al Simani and Yuhanna al Ujaimi.

4.1 Yusuf Simaan al Simani (1687–1768)

Al Simani was a graduate of the Maronite College in Rome. He served a number of popes and was accredited for writing a table of contents and a Latin conclusion for Oriental Manuscripts. Al Simani played a significant role in the Lebanese Council in 1736 which issued the Maronite fundamental law. He wrote several historical books and translated Greek books to the Latin language. He died in Rome in 1736. Al Simani is considered one of the most important pioneers in the intellectual awakening of the eighteenth century.[2]

Al Simani's purpose in writing is to defend his group, ascertaining its religious identity in its affiliation to the Antiochian Patriarchate and its constant allegiance to the Apostolic Chair. In his book *Nabdat fi silsilat Batarikat Madinat allah Antakiah*,[3] he relates information concerning the Maronite Patriarchs from the time of the Apostle Peter, who dwelled seven years in Antioch and was appointed patriarch before moving to Rome. He also mentions other orthodox and heretical patriarchs till he reaches after a period of seven centuries to Tuwafan, the last Melkite patriarch, who died in 685.

Al Simani states that the Maronite Patriarchate – "*the legal heiress to the Antiochian Patriarchate*" – starts after the death of Patriarch Tuwafan and with Yuhanna al Souroumi. This continues with a number of Orthodox Patriarchs who joined the Roman Chair, reaching

DOI: 10.4324/9781003023432-5

the times of Patriarch Yakoub Awwad al Hasrouni, who chaired the Patriarchate for 28 years till his death in 1733. Al Simani considers the Maronites since Yuhanna Maroun as the legal heirs to the Antiochian chair, affirming that the other Eastern Churches are not authentic and that they acquired this identity as an honorary title. Quoting Bishop Jibrail ben al Quilai, al Simani states that the Roman pope bestowed on Yuhanna Maroun the directorship of the Antiochian Patriarchate. This was also mentioned by other historians like Estephan al Duwaihi and others.[4]

Al Simani confirms that the Maronites are the Patriarchs of Antioch and not the Malikites,[5] for the pope confirmed these Patriarchs on the Antiochian Chair and not the Malikites, who succumbed to the heretical "one will" doctrine.

Al Simani was not confined to the Malikite patriarchs, but he also mentioned the Latin Patriarchs who chaired the Antiochian Patriarchate at the times of the Crusades. According to al Simani, the latter were not authentic patriarchs since they started in 1099 and were not heirs to the ancient patriarchs.[6]

Moving to the Maronite Question, al Simani states that after the murder of 500 priests in Mar Maroun convent in Syria, the destruction of the convent and the escape of Yuhanna Maroun and his companions to Lebanon, a number of wars occurred in this area, which ended in the defeat of the conquerors. *"Those who followed the king were called Malikites while those who continued under Patriarch Yuhanna Maroun were called Maronites."*[7] The Maronites were before called "al Marada" because they disobeyed Emperor Justinian.[8] Al Simani concludes that the election of Yuhanna Maroun as a Patriarch did not occur in the Antiochian Patriarchal Council, but in the Marada Council who disobeyed Emperor Justinian.

If we go back to Estephan al Duwaihi, we notice a different opinion on the Maronite question. He says: *"the right opinion which obliterates all ignorance is that the Maronites got their name from Maroun the hermit whose sanctity spread in the land of Quorus. This is how we are called Maronites."*[9] In another place, he adds that the Maronites got their name from the convent they lived in together with Yuhanna al Souroumi, the son of the French Aghaton and Anohamia.[10]

This is how al Simani defends his group affirming that the Maronite Patriarchate is the true Patriarchate and the legal heir to the Antiochian Patriarchate and that the Maronites are the only Catholic sect which was since its institution affiliated to and united with the Apostolic Chair. He provides several consecutive proofs to support his conviction.[11]

Apologetic History 59

Al Simani goes on defending his sect, offering proofs and quoting Jibrail ben al Quilai, Estephan al Duwaihi, and other Maronite historians.[12] In this he endeavors to rely on logic and gives proofs to confirm his beliefs and supports his argument while relying at the same time on Syriac and Latin sources and comparing between the different texts. Al Simani does not only chronicle the events, but he comments, analyses, and gives proofs. At the same time, he relates the biographies of the different historians as he did with Estephan al Duwaihi.[13]

Al Simani's endeavor to analyze, defend, and provide proofs prompted the other sects to react and argue concerning Yuhanna Maroun and the constant affiliation of the Maronites to the Apostolic Chair. This led to confronting the apologetic method in writing history by a contradicting style denying the pretensions, relying on the different sources while following the scientific method in verifying the events.

4.2 Yuhanna al Ujaimi (1724–1785)

Al Ujaimi was born in the village of Joun in Lebanon in 1724. He entered the Institute of Propagating the Faith in Rome in 1737 where he stayed nine years. He studied theology, philosophy, natural sciences, history, and law apart from the Greek, Latin, and Italian languages. He visited France in 1751 where he stayed for two years. In 1762, he built a church in his village by the name of Yuhanna al Mamadan. He died in Europe in 1785.[14]

Al Ujaimi is answering the questions of one of the Christians. He writes: "I received your question where you desire to know first about the Patriarch who chaired the Antiochian Patriarchate after Makarios and, secondly, if Yuhanna Maroun was the one who chaired the Antiochian Patriarchate or another Patriarch. Thirdly, if Yuhanna Maroun was a catholic or a heretic and if the Maronites got their name from Yuhanna Maroun or from another."[15]

The purpose of al Ujaimi is to reveal the reality about Maronite history to enlighten the Christians and at the same time to refute Maronite pretensions and defend his sect of the Roman Catholics.

Regarding Yuhanna Maroun, al Ujaimi writes: "He was ordained by Makarios (Patriarch Makarios the heretical),[16] followed the Monothelite heresy (one will in Christ), and became head of all those who adopted this doctrine. This is why all the Catholics and heretics and the rest of the sects considered the Maronites to be Monothelites. Makarios gathered an army and used weapons. Al Ujaimi mentions that Makarios fought the Melkites, the Roman Catholics, and when the ecumenical council condemned Patriarch Makarios, Tawfanus was ordained Patriarch in 681 and after him Iskandar, Thomas, and Jawergios. Al Ujaimi concludes the Maronite claim to proclaim Yuhanna Maroun on the Antiochian Chair after Tawfanus is false": Yuhanna Maroun was not mentioned with the Antiochian Patriarchate, neither with the Orientals nor with the Westerners, and the Maronites remained heretics till the coming of the Crusades to Antioch in 1098 when they elected Bernardos as their Patriarch in 1100, then Rodelphos, and then Imarikos who attracted the Maronites to the authentic faith and to the reunion with the Holy Roman Church."[17] Al Ujaimi adds that the Maronites returned to their previous caprice several times as in 1450 until they came back to God and to the true Catholic belief.[18]

Al Ujaimi says that at the time of Pope Innocent III, who was the first to deal with the Maronites, their Patriarch Irmia al Amshiti, their first Catholic Patriarch, went to Rome to prove his faith. The Pope honored him and he made him a member of the Fourth Lateran Council, which was in session in 1215.

Al Ujaimi quotes the sources to strengthen his point and resorts to logic to argue and prove historical facts. Here al Ujaimi was not content solely in recounting the events, but he analyzed these events expressing a comprehensive outlook in interpreting history while resorting to logic, philosophy, and theology to defend his convictions. This is how we see him asserting while debating with al Simani and the Maronite historians that the Antiochian Patriarchate which the Maronites are alleged to belong is an honorary patriarchate granted to them by the Apostolic Chair in the eighteenth century when they joined the Roman Catholic Church. Al Ujaimi adds that Yuhanna Maroun was the first Maronite Patriarch at the time of Tawfanos[19] and that King Yustinianos (Emperor Justinian II, described as "the heretical" by the Maronite historians), who fought the Maronites in Syria and Lebanon, was a lawyer in the Sixth Ecumenical Council and that all the historians who attacked his politics and rule did not mention that he was heretical.[20] According to al Ujaimi, Justinian fought the Maronites as heretics and not otherwise. He adds that the Maronites doubt other Christians' beliefs if they do not acknowledge the sanctity of Yuhanna Maroun and accuses Maronite historians of their failure in verifying their sources, but sought that their confession prove its allegiance to the Roman Church and its rapprochement with the French who were protecting them. Here al Ujaimi criticizes al Simani, mentioning that he wrote about the Eastern people clearly except what concerns the Maronites without including what proves Maronite heresy.[21] Al Ujaimi adds that any people or sect named after a personality is heretical.[22]

Al Ujaimi starts by answering one of the Christians soberly and vehemently at the same time, going through all the questions in order and obliterating what he considers against known historical facts. An example was his answer on the third question concerning Yuhanna Maroun. *"Maronites call Yuhanna Maroun Patriarch of Antioch and this is not true and a misconception to all those acquainted with the history of the Church. This is why before we describe the origin of this man and the reason for his name as a patriarch, we will give a biography of Maroun the hermit so that treason will be revealed."*[23]

After distinguishing between Maroun the hermit and Yuhanna Maroun (who he calls mutinous and his followers as villain hermits),[24] al Ujaimi relates the historical facts to prove his point of view, interacting and debating with historical Oriental, Latin, and French sources, while relying on Maronite historians to contradict them. He says that their disagreement as to the date of Yuhanna Maroun's patriarchate is greater for the one who is aware of the history of the Church. Al Quilai says that it was in 625, al Haqilani mentions the end of the sixth century and the beginning of the seventh, al Duwaihi mentions 676 as the beginning of his episcopate and his patriarchate at 688, while for al Simani it was in 658. In the same way, the local Lebanese Council considered Maroun's patriarchate to have been in the same year when Tawfanos passed away, considering this date as the safest. This discrepancy among the Maronite historians led some European scholars to conclude that there is no basis or reality for the existence of Yuhanna Maroun, thus concluding that this is pure fabrication that cannot be validated if verified in the realm of historical analysis and criticism.[25]

Al Ujaimi here mentions the principles of historical criticism revealing a sense of history and awareness of the need for objectivity in writing. He gives proofs using the accusation of the Maronites to verify his point of view, thus defending the testimony of Said ben al Batrick who is accused of distorting facts by the Maronites. He asserts that al Batrick ignored certain ancient historical facts which resulted by mistake in a few incorrect facts. If his history is mistaken in a few facts it does not entail that he is constantly incorrect. To prove his inaccuracy in the Maronite subject, he has to be compared to another historian not far from Yuhanna Maroun's century to be able to verify the facts. Here neither the testimony of al Duwaihi nor the knowledge of al Simani for historical knowledge depends mainly on testimony and recounting. Besides, what he ignored were matters that do not concern his times nor what was close to him. He wrote on what was known about the Maronites who were living at the same time in Lebanon. Al Ujaimi adds that the fact that the patriarch was not falsified for centuries is a proof of his truthfulness whereas the accusations of the belated Maronites are of no value unless they bring a convincing testimony.

Al Ujaimi delves into historical facts to prove his point of view giving an overall picture while searching for the truth. Knowledge alone is not sufficient, but of equal importance is integrity in presenting the evidence and copying the historical documents. Al Ujaimi stresses the importance of the Patriarch's contemporaries, not those who came in later centuries. Al Ujaimi is drawing attention to the importance of the historian's environment and the century he lives in as vital elements in evaluating historical facts.

This comprehensive view in verifying facts appeared while mentioning Yuhanna al Dimashqui. He writes: "There are some who support the teacher Simaan al Simani that these words attributed to Yuhanna al Dimashqui do not mean that the Maronites were heretical, but that he was not agreeing with them."[26]

Al Ujaimi seems confident of what he is presenting. He is not content solely in being acquainted with the sources, but he verifies, compares, and gives proofs to measure the realities. He uses induction and deduction to obliterate what the Maronite historians are contending. At the end of his dialectical method, he invites the Maronites to a dialogue and cooperation. He records:

> *"Some Maronites might think that we intend to dishonor them if we do not admit that Yuhanna Maroun is a saint or that they took their name from Saint Maroun, but this is not considered a shame with any Christian for we are all originally from the Jews who crucified Christ or from the pagans and now we are Christians and the descendants of the Christian Catholic Church so what is the dishonor in being originally from the pagans or the Jews...Where is the dishonor if the Maronites acknowledge that they were heretics and that Yuhanna Maroun is heretical and that the Maronites took his name in the past, for the Maronites have been for centuries part of the universal church and strongly affiliated to the Roman Holy See and as a result refusing all the heretical tendencies and taking Saint Maroun the hermit as their patron and are affiliated to him."*[27]

Al Ujaimi proceeds:

> "*Added to this, let them correspond with the Holy See and seek his judgement concerning Yuhanna Maroun. We are ready to consider Yuhanna Maroun among the Saints if he so decides no matter how this opinion might contradict the Western and Eastern scholars and historians. This is what we plan to explain to you, beloved son, about Yuhanna Maroun and the origin and condition of the Maronites, and in spite of all this we advise you and the rest of our community to keep with them the spirit of love and peace. We have constantly to collaborate with them since their faith is sincere and without blemish. Our Lord Jesus Christ is the Lord of us all.*"[28]

Al Ujaimi is objective in his argument, and he at the same time is ready to dialogue with the Maronites with the purpose of safeguarding Christian faith and not to defend a specific identity. His readiness to accept the opinion of the Holy See after presenting his arguments could be an indication of his humility in front of knowledge and authority and his openness in searching for the truth. Al Ujaimi and with him al Simani bestowed a special flavor on this historical controversy and crowned historical writing in that century.[29]

Notes

1. The Maronites were faced with repeated denials of their original and unbroken orthodoxy, so they defended it and went back to the story of their community in evidence. Maronite historiography developed partly as a by-product of polemics. See: Kamal Salibi, *Maronite Historians of Mediaeval Lebanon* (Beirut: American University of Beirut, 1959), 16.
2. See Yusuf al Dibs, *Al Jamih al Mufassal fi Tarikh al Mawarinat al Muassal* (Beirut: al Matbat al Kathulikiah, 1905), 483; also, Georg Graf, *Geschichte Der Christlichen Arabischen Literatur*, 111 and 444–455.
3. The book is 43 pages long.
4. Al Simani, *Nabdat*, 23; Jibrail ibn al Quilai was a Maronite historian who died in 1516. See Kamal Salibi, *Maronite Historians of Mediaeval Lebanon*, 1–82.
5. Or Melkites.
6. Al Simani, *Nabdat*, 25.
7. Al Simani, *Nabdat*, 35.
8. Al Simani, *Nabdat*, 32.
9. Estephan al Duwaihi, *Asl al Mawarinat*, ed. by Arwan Daou Ihdin (Manshurat al Turath al Ihdini, 1972), 1: 163.
10. Al Duwaihi, *Asl al Mawarinat*, 1: 113.
11. Al Simani, *Nabdat*, 33.

64 *Apologetic History*

12 On the Maronite historians, see Kamal Salibi, *Maronite Historians of Mediaeval Lebanon*, 13–22.
13 Al Simani, *Nabdat*, 2.
14 See Louis Cheikho, *Kitab al Makhtoutat al Arabiyya li Katabat al Nisraniyyah* (Beirut: Matbaat al Aba al Yasouiyyin, 1924), 146. Also, Georg Graf, *Geschichte Der Christlichen Arabischen Literatur* (Rome: Bibliotheca Apostolica Vaticana, 1949), 11, 177, 182, 237, 290, and 468.
15 Yuhanna al Ujaimi, *Al Hujja al Rahina fi haqiqat Asl al Muwarinat* (Cairo: Matbaat al Tamaddun, 1900).
16 See Stanley Mayes, *Makarios: a biography* (New York, NY: St Martin's Press, 1981).
17 Yuhanna al Ujaimi, *Al Hujja al Rahina*, 6–8.
18 Yuhanna al Ujaimi, *Al Hujja al Rahina*, 10–11.
19 Yuhanna al Ujaimi, *Al Hujja al Rahina*, 3.
20 Yuhanna al Ujaimi, *Al Hujja al Rahina*, 35.
21 Yuhanna al Ujaimi, *Al Hujja al Rahina*, 32–36.
22 Yuhanna al Ujaimi, *Al Hujja al Rahina*, 19.
23 Yuhanna al Ujaimi, *Al Hujja al Rahina*, 3–4.
24 Yuhanna al Ujaimi, *Al Hujja al Rahina*, 7.
25 Yuhanna al Ujaimi, *Al Hujja al Rahina*, 28–29.
26 He means adding the crucifixion to the Almighty God.
27 Al Ujaimi, *Al Hujja al Rahina*, 36–37.
28 Al Ujaimi, *Al Hujja al Rahina*, 39.
29 On Christian historians in general, see Kamal Salibi, *Maronite Historians of Mediaeval Lebanon*.

Reference List

Al Dibs, Yusuf. *Al Jamih al Mufassal fi Tarikh al Mawarinat al Muassal.* Beirut: al Matbat al Kathulikiah, 1905.

Al Duwaihi, Estephan *Asl al Mawarinat*, ed. by Arwan Daou Ihdin. Manshurat Ihdin, Lebanon. al Turath al Ihdini, 1972.

Al Simani, Rome. *Nabdat fi silsilat Batarikat Madinat allah Antakiah.*

Al Ujaimi, Yuhanna. *Al Hujja al Rahina fi haqiqat Asl al Muwarinat.* Cairo: Matbaat al Tamaddun, 1900.

Cheikho, Louis. *Kitab al Makhtoutat al Arabiyya li Katabat al Nisraniyyah.* Beirut: Matbaat al Aba al Yasouiyyin, 1924.

Graf, Georg. *Geschichte Der Christlichen Arabischen Literatur.* Rome: Bibliotheca Apostolica Vaticana, 1949.

Mayes, Stanley. *Makarios: a biography.* New York, NY: St Martin's Press, 1981.

Salibi, Kamal. *Maronite Historians of Mediaeval Lebanon.* Beirut: American University of Beirut, 1959.

Conclusion

This study is a panorama of a bygone century that has not been given its due in the history of ideas. It reveals historical thinking in the eighteenth century through the writings of the historians of that period – chroniclers, neo-chroniclers, autobiographers, biographers, and historians of apologetics – who tackled various subjects and gave a picture of a bygone period, revealing awareness of society in all its aspects – religious, political, intellectual, economic, social, and cultural – conveying a rich century and a stepping stone to future centuries.

To start with the chroniclers, one should observe that they gave an ample picture of the society they were living in. They delved into the various concerns of the people, relating the political, social, or religious events in their lives. In this sense, chronicle writing in the eighteenth century departed from two basic conceptions – religion and politics – and concentrated mainly on the ruling and upper strata in society, neglecting the lower classes except when mentioning the calamities of nature, famine, and epidemics. One has to mention here popular history that concentrated mainly on the lower strata of society and their daily concerns, presenting a liaison between the upper classes and the lower strata in society.

Chroniclers can be classified into three classes: the chroniclers who related the events, the neo-chroniclers who, while relating the events, analyzed and endeavored to find meaning and conclusions in what they encountered, and the historians of apologetics[1] who went beyond relating the events to think of causes and effects, searching for the truth of their origin, resorting to proofs, and employing logic to prove their points. It is here that Yusuf Siman al Simani and Yuhanna al Ujaimi delved into the picture. They concentrated on the Antiochian Patriarchate and eighteenth-century schisms in the church, conveying a picture of the apologetic scene while delving

66 *Conclusion*

into the subject of the origin of the Maronites and the issue of Mar Yuhanna Maroun.

Another form of historical writing in this period is biographical writing, which is reflected in both autobiography and biography. Abdallah Qarali, the founder of the Maronite monastic religious orders, conveyed an ample picture of life in the convents in that century while at the same time describing his personal development in the love of God. It is a story of a religious society and a road towards perfection at the same time. This religious society is conveyed with its virtues, problems, and intrigues to show that human frailty resides in the world and in the religious orders at the same time. Qaral's autobiography is a road toward perfection and finding oneself in the creator.

Coming to biography, we encounter Abbud al Sabbagh, who comes to the fore with his biography of the Muslim ruler Daher al Umar and his two associates, Ibrahim al Sabbagh and Ahmad Agha al Dinkizli. One is introduced to the political and social atmosphere of Palestine in that era. It is a biography of a ruler, presenting at the same time historical facts and information about the eighteenth century and the role played by the European powers in regional politics.

A few questions arise in this context:

Was the eighteenth century a period of stagnation in historical writing?

The eighteenth century was rich in its historians and their writings. These historians manifested interest in various subjects while relating events, analyzing them, and defending their convictions. These authors tackled various subjects, as in Hanania al Munayyir, Niqula al Turk, Yuhanna al Ujaimi, al Simani, and others.

These historians followed a method which obliterated the conception of a decadent and arid century. They explained, analyzed, and mentioned their sources and learned from the events. An example is Yusuf Siman al Simani and also Yuhanna al Ujaimi, who with their scientific approach quoted different sources, comparing and contrasting these sources and resorting to logical analysis to prove their points. At the same time, the historians were concerned in following the European method in their economy of using words while giving a full picture of the situation.

These historians, no doubt, did not possess a clear conception of history and lacked what is called *historiosophy*, that depart from the events, their causes and results, to the laws that dominated these events to show the causes for the rise and fall of nations and an understanding of the intervention of the eternal in history. They did, however, express a particular view in their endeavor to draw meaning and lessons from events while analyzing the controversies and defending their religious beliefs. This in itself can be understood as a nucleus to what is called the philosophy and theology of history and it obliterates the idea of a decadent eighteenth century.

Did a feeling of Lebanese identity develop in the eighteenth century?

The eighteenth century was a period of development and change. The struggle between the Ottoman Sultan and the Shah of Persia revealed the racist difference between the Turks and the Persians and nurtured a feeling among the Muslim Arab historians to be different from the Turks. This movement was centered around the Muslim scholars who defended the Arabic language and took pride in an authentic past.

This movement affected the Christians at the same time. They cooperated with the Muslims in spreading the Arabic language and in their interest in the culture of the past which fused to a great extent with Arabic culture. This aroused a sense of belonging among those writers to a special area which was expressed in different ways and led to a thrust among the enlightened communities to awaken them to their past and their identity.[2]

It is here that the feeling of Lebanese identity came to the fore among the different historians as with Abdallah Qarali, who called his order the "Lebanese Congregation" to distinguish it from the other religious orders. This feeling was extended further in al Aynturini, who seemed to believe in Lebanon not only as the mountain, but also in the south, the north, and the Biqa. This Lebanon was on the road to proving itself as an entity open to new boundaries in the process of developing into a country of its own. This was developed in Al Shihabi while describing Lebanon under the Shihabi Emirate. There he believed in an entity special in its setup and identity where nations came and departed to engender a multicultural and unique country with special characteristics of its own. And, lastly, this distinct Lebanese identity can be found in Hanania al Munayyir, where the picture of Lebanon is expressed in a glowing picture describing the Christian mountain as having strong relations with the West, and the Druze mountain with Christians living in its midst. He also describes the Beirut harbor alongside a mountain where Druzes, Muslims, and Christians lived together. He writes about Christian missionaries opening schools, about the silk production and other

68 Conclusion

activities which made Beirut a place of interaction in the area. Al Munayyir is not only proud of Lebanon, but he is at the same time aware of this entity which might collapse at any time.³

"Was the nineteenth century awakening a leap from void to existence, from sluggishness to vitality, from ignorance to knowledge and was this a new push in the structure of the Lebanese entity?"

These questions were no doubt dealt with in one way or another in our study. If the nineteenth-century awakening is the feeling of awareness among the historians of not belonging solely to their religious sect, but to their social and geographic environment as well, then this was found among the historians of the eighteenth century. Abbud al Sabbagh, for example, did not depart from a religious trend when writing about Daher al Umar, but he was secular in presenting the events in its political, social, and historical setting and at the same time presented the role of the al Sabbagh family while relating the events.

If the nineteenth-century awakening is understood as going beyond the local happenings to the events and situation in Europe, then this was manifested clearly in the writings of eighteenth-century historians like Rufail Karameh al Himsi, and Niqula al Turk. If, on the other hand, the awakening is understood to analyze the subjects, refer to European and Arab sources while comparing and contrasting the different writings, then one can refer to Yuhanna al Ujaimi and Siman al Simani, whose work demonstrated a development in historical writing at that time.

As for the sense of belonging to a specific area or particular people as a result of shared inherited culture and language, this was also manifested among eighteenth-century historians such as Rufail Karameh al Himsi, who expressed an attachment to Lebanon and called for unity among the different religions, calling for a solid basis in order to build a healthy Lebanon. This attachment to Lebanon was also manifested among other historians, as with al Aynturini, Haidar Shihab, al Munayyir, and others.

The aforementioned trends developed in the nineteenth century as a result of the interaction with new political, social, economic, and intellectual facts. In this sense, one can say that what happened in the nineteenth century was not a unique leap or a new push in the history of Lebanon, but a result of previous interactions and a historical necessity. Various nations left their imprints on Lebanese soil to nourish it and contribute to its advancement while being unable to obliterate its distinctive characteristic as a land that can fathom all cultures and adapt it to what befits its traditions and aspirations. This is how this land interacted since ancient times with different cultures, including Greek, Roman, Byzantine, Persian, Syriac, and Arabic. The European civilization, heir of the previous civilizations, had impacted Lebanon since the age of the Crusades. This interaction and influence developed with time in science, culture, commerce, and other areas and in the eighteenth century it was ready to burst out and give forth its fruits. This is how the emergence of the intellectual and national movements in the nineteenth century was not a result solely of the French Revolution and the ideas that accompanied it, but was as mentioned before, a result of historical interactions with ancient cultures who impacted Lebanon throughout the ages. The eighteenth century was peculiar in this interaction through the historians standing on the threshold pointing to a new era and awaiting its dawn to emerge. This is how the eighteenth century was laden with deep meanings and a long culture, similar to a bud in its simplicity unfolding into the flower and its fruit, a chain of future productions.

Notes

1 Historians of apologetics were placed in the study as a separate chapter and not with the chroniclers.
2 For the major trends in the eighteenth century, see: Albert Hourani, *The Fertile Crescent in the Eighteenth Century* (Beirut: Khayyat, 1962), 50–60.
3 Al Munayyir, *Al Durr* (1984), 127.

Reference List

Al Munayyir, Hanania. *Al-Durr al-Marsuf fi Hawadith al-Shuf*, ed. by Ignatius Sarkis. Beirut: Dar al Raid al Arabi, 1984.

Hourani, Albert. *The Fertile Crescent in the Eighteenth Century*. Beirut: Khayyat, 1962.

Index

Abbas, Sheikh 14
al Ahad, Abd (Abd Allah) 13
al Aynturini, Antonios Abu Khattar 10–13, 15; chronicle writing 10–12; loyalty to Maronites 13; *Mukhtasar Tarikh Jabal Lubnan* 10; sources for historical writing 10–11
al Azm, Ahmad Ibn 7
al 'Azm, Saad al Din Pasha 14
al Batrick, Said ben 61
al ᶜUmar, Zāher 8
al Dahab, Muhammad Abu 7–8
al Dinkizli, Ahmad Agha 49, 52
al Duwaihi, Estephan 59
al Duwayhi, Estephan 10
al Hasrouni, Patriarch Yakoub Awwad 58
al Himsi, Rufail Karameh 5–10, 15, 68; besiege of Beirut 8; events in Jabal 'Amel 15; feudal families' struggle for power 14; living conditions in monasteries 6–7; pilgrimages 15; politics and religion 6–8, 15
Ali, Muhammad 34
al Jazzar 8–9, 21–22, 34–35, 51
al Kabir, 'Ali 23
al Ma'ni, Ahmad 32
al Mi'zamieh, Wadi 14
al Munayyir, Hanania 9, 16, 19–26, 66; account of political situation 20–22, 25–26; *al Durr al Marsuf fi Hawadith al Shuf* 19; attitude toward women 22–23; *The History of the Religious Orders* 23;

Lebanese thinking and preoccupations 24; Mount Lebanon history 19; Ottoman interference in Lebanon 21; religious events 24; secular trend 22; writing style 21–23, 25–26
al Quilai, Bishop Jibrail ben 58–59
al Rukayni, Haydar Ibn Rida 13–15; *Jabal Amel fi Qarn* 14; Lebanese thinking, eighteenth century 15
al Sabbagh, Abbud 8, 49–53, 66, 68; *al Rawd al Zahir fi Tarikh Daher* 49, 53; as a biographer 52; biography of Daher al Umar 50–53; writing approaches 50
al Sabbagh, Ibrahim 23, 49, 52
al Sham, Bilad 3
al-Shidyak, Tannus 23
al Shihabi, Emir Bashir 12
al Shihabi, Haidar Ahmad 31–37; admiration for Napoleon and the French 35–37; *Al Ghurar al Hisan fir Akhbar Abna al Zaman* 32; on Emir Haidar 33; French expedition to Egypt 35–36; relations with Ottoman governors 32–34; Shihabs rule 34; writing style 31–32
al Shihābī, Yūsuf 7
al Simani, Yusuf Simaan 57–59, 62, 65–66, 68; on Malikite patriarchs 58; on Maronite Patriarchs 57–63; *Nabdat fi silsilat Batarikat Madinat allah Antakiah* 57; role in Lebanese Council 57
al Souroumi, Yuhanna 57

al Turk, Niqula 26–31, 66, 68; contrast between East and West 30; difference between French and Egyptian customs and language 29–31; on French Revolution and rise of Napoleon Bonaparte 27–29; portrayal of European in Egyptian society 29–31; repugnance of Muslims 29
al Ujaimi, Yuhanna 59–63, 65–66; historical knowledge 62; on Makarios 59–60; on Yuhanna Maroun 59
al 'Umar, Daher 21, 23, 49–53
al 'Umar, Zaher 7, 14
'Amel, Jabal 15
Antiochian Patriarchate 57–60, 65
apologetic history and historians 2–3; al Simani, Yusuf Simaan 57–59; al Ujaimi, Yuhanna 59–63
Arabic Historical Thought in the Classical Period (al Khalidi) 1
The Art of Biography (Woolf) 42
autobiographers 1, 3; Qarali, Abdallah 42–49

Badrān, Abi Antūn 7
Bashir II 10, 19, 21, 24
Bashir II, Emir 31
Batn, Yusuf Ibn 13
Battle of Abukir 36
Battle of Ain Dara, 1711 11, 20
Battle of Ayndara, 1711 33
Baz, Jurjus 35
Beirut seizure 8
Bey, Ali 50–51
Bey, Ibrāhīm 29
Beydoun, Dr. Ahmad: *Identité Confessionnelle et Temps Sociale Chez les Historiens Libanais Contemporains* 24
Binyamin of Ihdin, Jirjis 47
biographers/biographical writing 1–3, 42; al Sabbagh, Abbud 49–53
Bishara, Bilad 14
Bkirki monastery 6
The Blooming Garden in the History of Daher 53

Bonaparte, Napoleon 35–37; expedition to Egypt, 1798 8, 21, 27, 35
Breik, Mikhail 7–8

Catherine the Great 9
Catholics 1, 6–7, 9–10, 22, 24, 27, 58–60
Christianity/Christians 1, 6–7, 9, 23, 27, 29, 34
chroniclers/chronicle writing 1–3, 15; al Aynturini, Antonios Abu Khattar 10–13; al Rukayni, Haydar Ibn Rida 13–15; classification 65
Church of the Hill *(Kanisat al-tallah)* 23

Dahab, Abu'l 23; seizure of Beirut 23
Dayr al-Qamar 23, 27
Druze-Christian relations 7–8, 24, 34
Druzes 1

el Bizri, Dr. Nader 3
Elisha, Mar 47
Emirs of the Mountain 7

Farhat, Jibrail 47
French Revolution 27, 69

Greek Catholics 5–7, 9–10, 22, 24, 27

Hamadeh Shii family 12
Harafishah family 7
Hawwa, Jibrail 13, 44, 46–47, 54n8
Hindiyyah 6
historians of dialectics 1
historiography and historians of Lebanon 1, 66–67; autobiographers 1, 3; biographers 1–3; chroniclers 1–3; eighteenth century 2–3, 66–69; historians of apologetics 3; neo-chroniclers 1, 9

Imara (Emirate), political affairs of 19

Kleber, General 37

72 *Index*

Lebanese identity 2–3, 46, 67–68

Maronites 1–2, 10–11, 13, 20, 43, 58, 60–63, 66; Maronite monastic orders 43, 46, 66; religious life 13
Maroun, Patriarch Yuhanna 58–61
Mikhail, Emperor 9
Mount Lebanon history 19, 22
Moura, Hawwa Mar 47
Mukhtasar Tarikh Jabal Lubnan 11
Muscovites 9
Muslims 2, 9, 26, 29–30, 36, 38n22

Nassif, Sheikh 14
neo-chroniclers 1, 9, 16, 65; al Munayyir, Hanania 19–26; al Shihabi, Haidar Ahmad 31–37; al Turk, Niqula 26–31

Ottomans 9, 15, 21; war between Muscovites and 9

Parker, Dr. Scott 3
Pasha, Ibrahim 34

Qarali, Abdallah 42–49; as an autobiographer 48; as a biographer 48; communal life in monasteries 43; founding of Maronite monastic orders 43, 46; as a historian 47; memoirs 48–49; on Patriarch Awwad's tendencies and personality 45; self-awareness 44–46; use of analogy 48
Qaysi Yamani–Yazbaki Jumblati struggle 20–21

religious society 6–7, 13, 43, 66. *see also* Maronites
Rotberg, Robert 42

sacerdotal order 6
schismatic Rum 6–7
Shihab, Haidar 20
Shihabi family 11
Shihāb II, Bashīr 27
Shi'ites 1, 34
Sixth Ecumenical Council 60
Smith, Sidney 7, 21–22, 36
society of Lebanon 5–6
St. Elias (the Prophet Elijah) 7
Sultan of the Tartars 9
Sunnis 1, 34

Tuwafan, Patriarch 57

Yamanites' expulsion 20
Yustinianos, King 60
Yusuf, Emir 12

For Product Safety Concerns and Information please contact our EU representative GPSR@taylorandfrancis.com
Taylor & Francis Verlag GmbH, Kaufingerstraße 24, 80331 München, Germany

www.ingramcontent.com/pod-product-compliance
Lightning Source LLC
Chambersburg PA
CBHW051800230426
43670CB00012B/2369